INSIDE
WHOLE LANGUAGE

a classroom view

Hazel Brown & Vonne Mathie

Primary English Teaching Association
NSW, Australia

Heinemann
Portsmouth, New Hampshire

Heinemann Educational Books, Inc.
361 Hanover Street   Portsmouth, NH 03801
Offices and agents throughout the world

Copyright © Primary English Teaching Association, 1990
PO Box 167   Rozelle NSW 2039 Australia

First U.S. printing 1991

Library of Congress Cataloging-in-Publication Data
Brown, Hazel, 1943-
      Inside whole language : a classroom view / Hazel Brown & Vonne
  Mathie

          p.   cm.
      Reprint. Originally published: 1990.
      Includes bibliographical references (p.   ).
      ISBN 0-435-08583-2
      1. Language experience approach in education.   2. Activity
  programs in education.   3. Reading (Primary)--Language experience
  approach.   I. Mathie, Vonne, 1947-   . II. Primary English
  Teaching Association (Australia) III. Title.
  LB1576.B85   1991
  372.4'144--dc20   90-26936
                                                                  CIP

Cover design by Gordon Baine
Edited and designed by Jeremy V. Steele
Design consultant: Mark Jackson
Typeset in 11^{1}/2/13 by Tensor Pty Ltd
40-44 Red Lion Street Rozelle NSW 2039

Printed in the United States of America
91 92 93 94 95 9 8 7 6 5 4 3 2 1

WITHDRAWN

CONTENTS

PREFACE

We wanted to write a book about whole language learning in primary schools which would be used both by whole language practitioners and by newcomers to the concept. So we decided to start with our own basic beliefs and understandings about language and learning and then show how we program and organise and evaluate. The result is a 'Show and Tell' type of book in which we give practical interpretations of theory, lesson plans that work, advice on strategies to promote learning and examples of how we program and evaluate that learning. However, the two classrooms we describe should be seen only as workable examples which are by no means prescriptive. Our hope is that the book will act as a catalyst to trigger individuals into devising programs which suit their own needs and, more importantly, the needs of the children they teach.

Over the past five or six years we have worked extensively on whole language with primary school teachers, providing workshops and inservice courses throughout NSW and other States. In these we have tried to cater for teachers' needs and have therefore covered a wide area: organisation, strategies, evaluation, getting started, the reading-writing connection, pupils with special needs, the reluctant student, components of language lessons, language across the curriculum and so on. The teachers attending these courses have invariably asked for the information to be documented so that it might serve as a resource for themselves and for other teachers in their schools who couldn't attend.

So this book has partly been written for them — for teachers who are keen to join the whole language movement and need a starting point to help them put theory into practice. But it is also a book for teachers who have tried whole language and experienced problems they couldn't overcome. We too have 'been there and done that' — we have experienced many problems both of interpretation and implementation. But we are still hanging in there, thrilled with the outcome: the kids who have shown us the power of whole language learning; who talk and write with such verve and enthusiasm, and who make reading, writing and talking an integral part of learning in all curriculum areas. This book is about them and, via teachers, for them.

ACKNOWLEDGEMENTS

This book could not have been written without the support of the following friends:

Brian Cambourne, who has inspired so many teachers with his research, his commitment to literacy development and his generosity in sharing his findings.

Jan Turbill, who persuaded us that we could write a book that other teachers would want to read, and kept on believing in us.

Alison Yarrow, a terrific librarian, typical of all the unsung heroes of schools, whose knowledge and advice about children's literature are greatly appreciated.

Roy Williams, an enthusiastic colleague and a caring friend, who gave so willingly of his time and expertise.

Beryl Wood, who was that 'significant other' to a novice in the Kindergarten classroom.

The children of Balarang, Albion Park Rail, Warrawong and Nowra East Public Schools, from whom we have learned.

Jeremy Steele, our long-suffering editor, for whose advice we are ever grateful.

Gwen Mathie, a special mum, who provided encouragement, support and many culinary delights.

Eric Brown, whose understanding has sustained us.

Chapter One

BEHAVIOUR IS A REFLECTION OF BELIEFS

Why we became whole language teachers

In the early 1980s an exciting concept called Process Writing emerged in Australia. It arrived following the persuasive arguments of Donald Graves in America that writing should not be seen as something to be produced once a week in 'composition' class, but rather as a process of composing meaning. Jan Turbill and PETA supported this new approach to the teaching of writing with practical books and these were enough to draw us into the process movement. The results were exciting: the children became highly motivated and they learnt and understood much more about the process of writing. We too changed significantly during this period as we stopped teaching punctuation, spelling and grammar as ends in themselves, and came to see them rather as tools necessary for effective written communication.

At the same time as this was happening we still adhered to old-style reading lessons, but the excitement so obvious in writing was not there. It didn't take us long to realise the enormous disparities in what we were doing with the children. With a great deal of encouragement and support from Brian Cambourne, we became converted to a whole language approach to literacy learning. We stopped fragmenting language and started teaching it in much the same way as oral language is learned — as a whole. As with our early ventures into process writing, the results were very soon apparent. Attitudes towards reading and books generally improved. Children rapidly developed some expertise about the ways books are presented, about authors, style and interpretation. They spent more time reading, borrowed more and selected better. They talked about their reading and ideas spilled over into their writing. Our conversion was confirmed, and we are now convinced that there is no better way to teach language, both oral and written, than through a 'whole' approach.

Issues we had to resolve

Transforming ourselves from traditional-type teachers to more comfortable, confident, whole language teachers was not easy, nor did it happen overnight. It took a lot of soul-searching, talking, reading, trialling, making mistakes and trying again before we were satisfied that we really had a good thing going. What follows is a summary of some of the issues we had to resolve during our metamorphosis to establish our basic beliefs and understandings about literacy learning. None of these issues was so apparent at the time as they are now with the assistance of hindsight and reflection. But maybe you will identify with some of our problems and sympathise.

Literacy — what is it?

The most basic understanding we had to clarify concerned the notion of literacy. For a long time society has had a rather narrow definition of literacy. It has been perceived as the ability to read and write, to spell correctly, to punctuate a sentence conventionally ... and little else. And in such an atmosphere teachers have taught language in a narrow, trivialised and fragmented way, concentrating on the 'basics' (spelling, punctuation, grammar, etc.) and often divorcing them from writing.

We believe that there is far more to literacy than this. We define literacy as *the making of meaning and its clear communication to others.* We therefore believe that truly literate people not only can read and write, but regularly do so in order to sort out their ideas and put them in words, to fit them together and test hypotheses — in other words, to make sense and meaning out of our world. Truly literate people acknowledge that they *need* to write things down, to talk them out, to read widely, to listen critically and to respond articulately. Truly literate people are thinkers and learners.

And of course this view of literacy carries with it further implications, notably some centred on the permanency or durability of these skills and attitudes. We are all only too aware of the kind of people Cambourne calls 'dependent a-literate' learners: people who can read and write but who choose not to, people who are alienated from any sustained literacy acts and read and write only for functional reasons.

Why is our society full of such people? Why do we have such an abundance of wasted potential? Maybe the system is at fault. If reading and writing are taught and learned mechanically and without enthusiasm, children will not come to see their inherent value. We need to search out ways of making literacy learning more enjoyable and purposeful so that reading and writing become as durable as talking, and children are shown the possibilities for learning which hinge upon proficient use of language.

How do we promote durable literacy?

This is a question to which we certainly don't presume to have a complete answer. But we have arrived at some suggestions for encouraging a more positive attitude towards language and learning and these are definitely good starting points. We know that effective language teachers take account of them.

1: *Let the learning of language be uncomplicated*

Traditionally, western education has complicated the learning of language by fragmenting it into its four modes (talking, listening, reading and writing), and then by further fragmenting these into smaller sub-sets and sub-units. So, for example, writing was broken up into grammar, spelling and punctuation, all taught as discrete units divorced from their natural context. Such teaching was based on the belief that in order to understand 'big bits' like writing, one first had to understand or get control of the 'little bits' like spelling. However, when a parallel is drawn from learning to talk — itself a most complex task, where lots of language structures (initial sounds, blends, pronunciations, grammar, words, phrases, sentences, statements, questions, etc.) are juggled and co-ordinated and learned beautifully by very young children — the argument for fragmenting written language learning doesn't stand up. We believe that fragmentation complicates language learning unnecessarily; it makes it artificial.

Our belief is supported by Carolyn Burke (1984), whose concept of the Linguistic Data Pool explains the ever increasing pool of knowledge which language users carry around in their heads.

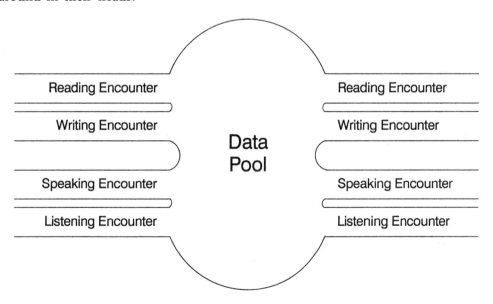

Reading Encounter   Reading Encounter
Writing Encounter   Writing Encounter
Data Pool
Speaking Encounter   Speaking Encounter
Listening Encounter   Listening Encounter

Every language encounter we have helps to fill this pool of knowledge, and the inflow can be drawn upon when we engage in another encounter. So, a child may listen to a story read by the teacher, later retell that story to another child and maybe even write a personal version.

Our experience as teachers has provided many similar instances of direct flow, and also many examples of what can be called 'linguistic spillover' (Brown & Cambourne 1987). These range from ideas, words and phrases to plots and particular features of a text which find their way from one language experience into another. We've often noticed vivid words or phrases 'lifted' (usually subconsciously) from stories read or heard and emerging orally or in written work.

Obviously, if all modes of our language are so interdependent and interwoven, to cut them apart and shred the pieces destroys their connectedness and hinders the development of the child's competent control of language.

2: *Let language learning be meaningful*

If our ultimate goal is to help students to use and enjoy their skills in language after formal schooling has ceased, then we have to ensure that their use of language at school has meaning for *them*. They must go beyond using language for simple functional reasons. While we do develop language control for this part of our lives — reading recipes, filling out forms, holding conversations — language has more powerful functions, particularly in the development of thinking, learning and imagination. And in order to develop understandings, knowledge and vision, we need to *use* language in all its four modes.

Language is both the process and the tool of learning. It is active and activated in all disciplines. It is exclusive to none. It must have practice in all disciplines to develop and communicate ideas. Every discipline is dependent upon it. It is the common ground of all.

Traditionally, as a result of concentrating on test results which would show what children had 'learnt', we have taught with a stress on learning content rather than on the development of thinking, perception and understanding. This sort of teaching was based on repetitive exercises rather than on problem-solving skills. But we can teach a parrot to recite the northern rivers of NSW. *This kind of teaching, we believe, has done nothing for learning.*

In order to make language learning meaningful we must foster an ethic of understanding: we must help students learn how to formulate and question hypotheses, how to locate information, how to sift and make sense of it, how best to communicate it. It is our responsibility to demonstrate these skills and processes and show children how to tackle the different kinds of information they will be exposed to. They will need all of these skills to be literate in a society that is changing rapidly and generating ideas at an ever accelerating pace.

3: *Help children to learn the craft of the author*

Children are in control when they can read and write competently. The person who is most in control is one knows *how* writing is used to communicate most effectively. This skill we refer to as author craft.

Author craft, as used by Donald Graves (1983), refers to the work involved in moulding, shaping or crafting a piece of writing until it reaches a satisfactory stage of completion. It is analogous to a potter shaping clay. However, we believe author craft includes more than this. Potters not only mould the clay, they need to know which is the most suitable clay for their purpose, where to locate it and how to dig it out. So language users need to know where to find the raw materials of their work, i.e. ideas, and be able to sort out which are relevant before crafting, or changing their form to suit the new purpose. Author craft, then, for us includes reading, reflecting, discriminating, note taking, discussing, summarising, generalising ... These strategies are common to all subject areas.

Ultimately learners, who are apprentice craftsmen, must learn to 'read like writers' by engaging with demonstrations and learning from them. They should then begin to 'write like readers', i.e. write with an audience in mind. This is what children need to be able to do if they are to become competent writers. Author craft is not simply concerned with producing or shaping a text; it is concerned with *acknowledging what has been done in effective text and using this text as a model for your own writing.*

4: *Expose children to a range of genres*

If children are to cope adequately in our rapidly changing society, they need the knowledge and understanding to be able to read, write and speak in a range of genres. This requires teachers to demonstrate by reading and by modelled writing the distinguishing features of each genre. From such demonstrations children will learn about the language features of the genre, the audience it targets, and the characteristics of its form or layout. Practice will consolidate this learning, but we need to plan for it and not assume it will happen incidentally.

5: *Promote a love of reading and writing*

It is our experience that children like to model themselves on someone they admire; someone who has assumed significance in their lives. The teacher is, or should be, such a person. If we as teachers are seen in class to enjoy books and to write, and if we talk about the satisfaction that these experiences give us, then we are providing a positive model for our students. 'Do as I do' is a powerful message, even when it is delivered indirectly.

6: *Provide a safe, stimulating learning environment*

When children learn to talk it is rarely hard or stressful and the success rate is enormous — not many of us could name someone who failed to learn to talk. One of the most significant factors in learning anything well is a supportive, non-threatening environment where pressure is reduced to a minimum and support is taken for granted. This is the sort of environment in which a child learns to talk. It is the kind of environment teachers must provide in classrooms. Children must want to be there because it is a happy, stimulating educational and social experience, a context where they are never bored, nor unnecessarily pressured, and where their learning is celebrated and has purpose.

Conclusion

Whatever we as teachers believe and understand about language and learning will underlie everything that occurs in our classrooms. It will affect the resources we collect, the teaching/learning methods we employ, the way we speak to children, how we interact with them and how we assess and evaluate their progress and control of language.

Chapter Two

THE CONDITIONS CONDUCIVE TO LEARNING

This chapter sets out our personal beliefs about how children learn language within the framework of Cambourne's Model of Learning. It is not our intention to give a systematic explanation of the theory supporting this model — it has been documented extensively elsewhere (notably in Cambourne 1988), and in addition forms the basis of *Writing K-12* (NSW Department of Education). Rather we wish to share our ideas about how the theory may be interpreted in the classroom.

In order to do so we have artificially teased apart Cambourne's conditions for learning and treated each one separately, following the same pattern. First we say what each condition means to us in terms of the whole language classroom. Then we outline the understandings that flow from our basic definition and describe some of the ways in which these understandings are realised in our classroom practice.

Immersion

For our purpose, immersion refers to ***the QUANTITY aspect of an effective learning environment.***

OUR UNDERSTANDING IS THAT ...

Learning takes place more easily when learners are constantly involved in a wide variety of stimulating language experiences appropriate to their needs. This constancy of involvement can also be expressed in terms of the other learning conditions.

- *Demonstrations* (both planned and spontaneous) are a vital component of *every* language session.

- Sufficient time for *practice* is allowed for *daily*.

- *Approximations* — without fear of criticism — are *regularly* encouraged.

- Positive *feedback* is given *continually*.

- Teacher language and actions *continually* indicate teacher *expectations* to the learner.

- Numerous opportunities for learners to accept more and more *responsibility* for their learning are provided *daily*.

Demonstration

For our purpose, demonstration refers to **the multitude of examples, both written and oral, which a learner needs in order to develop language control.**

OUR UNDERSTANDING IS THAT ...

Demonstration is a powerful teaching tool. Thus we plan demonstrations carefully so that we communicate clearly what we intend children to learn, and we try to take advantage of all teaching moments thrown up in language lessons.

Demonstrations should be programmed but also can be and often are spontaneous. Demonstrations to meet general class needs, such as reading a flow chart or exploring the conventions of fairy tale language, should be pre-planned carefully. However, every teacher is aware of times in a lesson when unforeseen needs arise and an impromptu demonstration is required. This may involve one child, a small group or the whole class — 'Please everyone stop and listen to me ...'

Demonstrations should be planned in response to identified needs. We therefore circulate daily to find out what specific needs the children have. For instance, if we find most children writing 'I sr a ...' (I saw a ...), there is obviously a real need for a demonstration to show everyone the conventional spelling.

Demonstrations should be an integral part of each daily language session, though they shouldn't take too long — 10-15 minutes is plenty. But we do need to identify whole class, group and individual needs, and program and teach accordingly.

Demonstrations should be meaningful. We have found that children appreciate a demonstration more when they are given the reason for it — for instance:

> 'I've noticed that most of you have been experimenting with limerick writing, so I think that maybe we can all look at limericks and work out a way to get the beat and rhyme right.'

> 'When you get to High School you're going to be asked to write a lot of reports. I think you should start learning now. I'm going to show you how I do it.'

A child helps Vonne Mathie to focus on the conventions of print during shared reading.
Children can give demonstrations by themselves too.

Demonstrations can be provided by a variety of people. These include the class teacher, children (peers) within the class, other staff members, children from other classes, and community members. In our experience, it's often better to send a child having problems to another child for help.

Demonstrations need to be repeated. We realise that not all children learn from a one-off demonstration. Language is complex and aspects need to be revisited regularly in further demonstrations — sometimes involving the whole class, sometimes just small groups or individuals. Demonstrations can also be reinforced by using environmental print and referring to it regularly, and by using opportunities thrown up during shared reading.

Demonstrations should be planned in all areas of the curriculum. All curriculum areas are language based, but certain genres are used more frequently in some than in others. Consequently children need demonstrations of the genres and language patterns characteristic of specific curriculum areas.

Teachers' actions and speech are demonstrations of their values and beliefs about language learning. For instance, a teacher who applauds a child's attempts to solve a problem before asking for help is demonstrating that this is preferred behaviour.

All print resources are demonstrations of how language is structured and used. We therefore direct learners to examples of accepted language use in classroom books and environmental print. Or, when we are using Big Books, we might demonstrate the conventions of print, or the effectiveness of a clearly labelled diagram.

Feedback (Response)

For our purpose, feedback refers to *the responses learners get from both teacher and other learners about their oral and written language development.*

OUR UNDERSTANDING IS THAT ...

Feedback is a response to a need. This need may be for encouragement, confirmation, reinforcement or redirection.

Feedback needs to be regular. Consequently a teacher should make daily contact with each learner.

Feedback must be constructive: it should confirm or promote learning. 'Success breeds success', and learners need to be aware of their own achievements. Self-esteem is very vulnerable. We don't always recognise the effort which has been put into work, nor see the agony and frustration endured by battlers. It's better not to say anything if we can't be constructive. However, the better we know children, the more our expectations of them are refined — and all of us know when we can legitimately say, 'This is not the best you can do.'

We always try to provide a moving-on point when responding to a child with a problem:

'Have you tried ...?'

'Go and speak to ...'

'Why don't you look at ...?'

Feedback is individual and so the teacher needs to know each learner intimately. There is really no substitute for child watching. Knowledge of individual children colours our expectations of them and determines the way we speak to them and what we say.

Feedback is not confined to conferences and structured sharing times. It is an ongoing, constant part of the daily interaction within classrooms and comes from other learners as well as the teacher.

Expectation

For our purpose, expectation refers to *the messages, both subtle and overt, which teachers communicate to their pupils about learning and learning behaviours.*

OUR UNDERSTANDING IS THAT ...

Expectations are conveyed by the ways in which teachers act, talk and behave. Learners will respond to these messages — as when they see their teacher use a dictionary to check a doubtful spelling during a writing demonstration.

Expectations should be positive.

'I know you can do it because I've been watching you write. You've got almost all of your story in proper sentences. How's about having a go at the rest? I'll help you if you get stuck, but you have a go first.'

Expectations must be realistic.

'You should be able to find the illustrator of *Possum Magic* because the book is on the shelf.'

Teacher expectations set the ground rules. For example, children in a sharing session may be expected to have prepared themselves and to be ready to answer questions.

Expectations are different for each child. Teachers need to be aware of each child's capabilities. They can best cultivate this awareness by interacting daily with each child in different learning situations.

Expectations set the learning climate in the classroom.

'I'm going to support you when you have a go, but you have to try too.'

Responsibility

For our purpose, responsibility refers to *that stage in the learning process when the learner says, 'Yes, it's up to me. I must take responsibility for learning this — no-one can do it for me.'*

OUR UNDERSTANDING IS THAT ...

Responsibility is akin to self-motivation. Accepting responsibility is a vital part of gaining independence in learning.

Learners should accept responsibility before engaging in the act of learning. Learning occurs best when learners decide what they will master.

Teachers can convey expectations through their choice of language and give children responsibility for learning and decision-making. Often teachers remove responsibility from children by telling rather than questioning. For instance, if insufficient information is causing problems in a piece of writing, don't say so to the child. Say rather, 'You tell me you are having difficulty with this piece. What do *you* think is the problem?'

Practice

For our purpose, practice refers to *the regular use of all aspects of oral and written language (talking, listening, reading and writing).*

OUR UNDERSTANDING IS THAT ...

In order to develop positive attitudes towards learning, learners must be allowed to practise their developing control of language without the threat of criticism. We therefore try to create the kind of environment where children feel free to 'have a go', and where we value and applaud their attempts.

The more learners practise, the greater their chances of achieving control. Accordingly we provide time every day to read, write and discuss.

The time needed for practice will vary for each child. We must allow for this in our language organisation. It is part of effective classroom management, but it does mean that we must know children well.

Practice in learning oral and written genres should occur in all the curriculum areas. All curriculum areas are language based. However, each of them has a different bias or focus, and certain genres need promotion in each one.

A learner needs positive feedback in order to realise the significance of practice. We therefore make a point of speaking frequently to each child about the progress we can see occurring in his or her reading and writing.

Practice is the context of approximation. Approximations may manifest themselves in the product, or during sharing and conference times.

Immersed in classroom print to check the spelling of 'kookaburra': children can take responsibility for their own learning at an early age.

Practice should occur at school and at home. We encourage children to read and write at home. We meet with parents to discuss this and help them to see their place in encouraging learning at home.

Approximation

For our purpose, approximation refers to *the learner's attempts to gain control of language, i.e. 'temporary language', 'near misses'.*

OUR UNDERSTANDING IS THAT ...

The teacher must see mistakes as a natural part of learning and not as features which have to be ruthlessly rooted out. We expect that mistakes in writing will be eliminated when children become aware of them and understand the need to standardise what they write. Similarly, mistakes in reading will be eliminated when children expect what they read to make sense.

Language is a complexity of structures. These vary from initial sounds and letters to completed stories, to critiques and analyses, to .... It's not possible for a learner to find a way through such complexity without sometimes misjudging and falling over. The sensitive teacher knows what aspect to help with and takes care not to overload the child's capacity to learn.

So, when helping a child, we concentrate on *one* aspect or approximation only — establishing meaning *always* takes priority. We select the approximation the child is closest to controlling and demonstrate the accepted form or usage within the context of the child's own work. What we are doing is accepting the approximation as a marker of development.

Approximations occur in all areas of language learning. Many teachers do not see beyond the approximations which occur in spelling. We have learned to expect them not only in spelling but in all areas of language development — for example:

- maintaining correct tense
- sound/symbol (phonic) relationships
- reading ('house' for 'home' is very different from 'house' for 'horse')
- sentence structure
- genre format.

Teachers should encourage learners to approximate and be adventurous in using language. We encourage a 'have-a-go' attitude, because children need to take risks in order to push out into the wider world of language control. Children who have a go are motivated and keen to learn. Their writing is more imaginative and wide-reaching than the writing of children who are taught that correctness is of paramount importance. Which of these two examples shows the more competent language use?

The fat cat sat on a red mat.

The catplla ws camufld on a gren lef.

We also talk about and demonstrate how we have a go, checking the result when we have more time, or find someone who can help us.

An approximation indicates a need requiring a demonstration. We keep alert to the ways children use language in our classrooms. Their approximations tell us what we need to demonstrate, and by responding to these needs we help them move from 'temporary language' to acceptable standard English.

Engagement

For our purpose, engagement refers to *that moment in the learning process when understanding occurs.*

OUR UNDERSTANDING IS THAT ...

Engagement is not a condition which can be consciously engineered. It is the ultimate act which the teacher strives for. It is preceded by the learner's acceptance of responsibility for learning and will be evidenced in the learner's use of language, both oral and written.

Engagement is fostered by plenty of demonstrations in a stimulating, supportive, non-threatening environment. Creating and maintaining this kind of learning environment depends on having realistic expectations and giving positive feedback.

Interdependence of the conditions

Although we have focused on each learning condition separately, it is well to remember that when a learning environment is functioning effectively, the learning conditions operate concurrently; they overlap, intertwine and are dependent upon one another. Indeed, in such an environment, they cannot function independently.

To illustrate their interdependence these conditions are often organised in diagrams which vary according to their intent and focus. The diagram overleaf shows the interdependence of the conditions when *demonstration* is the focus.

Demonstrations should be planned in response to needs identified via *practice*, *approximations*, *feedback* and *expectations*.

Demonstrations can provide *feedback* for and indicate *expectations* to the learner.

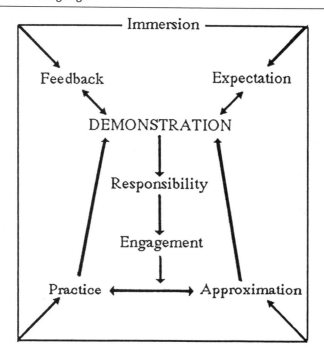

Responsibility is akin to self-motivation and must be accepted before a learner *engages* in the act of learning.

Practice can indicate the degree of *engagement.*

Practice is the context of *approximations.*

An *approximation* is a marker of development and indicates a need requiring a *demonstration.*

Immersion is the quantity aspect of an effective learning environment, where the conditions are operating at their optimum level.

Chapter Three

BELIEFS TRANSLATED INTO CLASSROOM PRACTICE

> *Children cannot be taught to read. A teacher's responsibility is not to teach children to read but to make it possible for them to learn to read.*
> (Smith 1983)

Smith's dictum may be applied to all language learning.

> Children cannot be taught language. A teacher's responsibility is not to teach children language but to make it possible for them to learn language.

But if *this* is our responsibility, how do we organise our classrooms, our programs and our time so that language learning is a possibility for all children? In this chapter we attempt to share with you our answers to that question:

- by identifying and elaborating upon the features which we believe are common to all whole language classrooms
- by demonstrating how these features are modified in order to respond to the specific needs of two different classes, in one of which (a Year 4 class) the majority of children have much greater language control than those in the other (a Kindergarten class)
- by describing a daily language session in each classroom.

We will begin by discussing the common features of whole language classrooms, which are shown in the diagram overleaf.

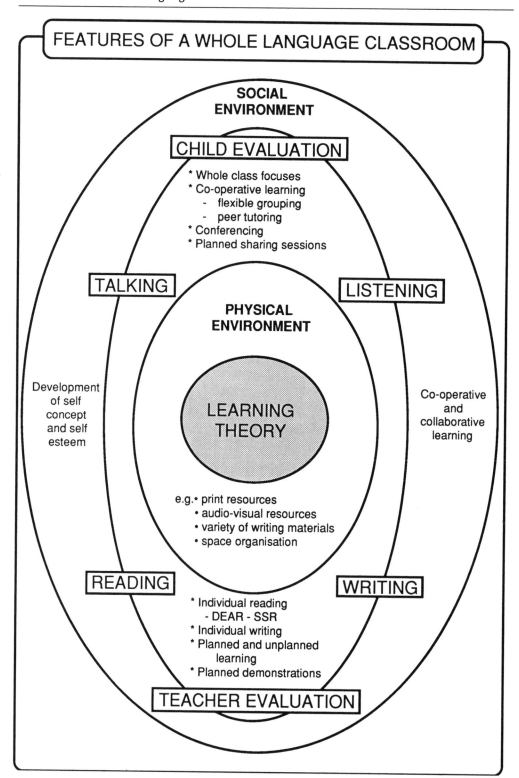

FEATURES OF A WHOLE LANGUAGE CLASSROOM

SOCIAL ENVIRONMENT

CHILD EVALUATION

* Whole class focuses
* Co-operative learning
   - flexible grouping
   - peer tutoring
* Conferencing
* Planned sharing sessions

TALKING

LISTENING

PHYSICAL ENVIRONMENT

LEARNING THEORY

Development of self concept and self esteem

Co-operative and collaborative learning

e.g.• print resources
   • audio-visual resources
   • variety of writing materials
   • space organisation

READING

WRITING

* Individual reading
   - DEAR - SSR
* Individual writing
* Planned and unplanned learning
* Planned demonstrations

TEACHER EVALUATION

Learning theory

Learning theory should provide the basis for determining both the content and the teaching, learning and evaluation strategies for the class program; i.e. it should be at the heart of teaching practice. Consequently classroom teachers should be able to:

- state their personal beliefs about how children learn, and, in particular, about how children learn language

- elaborate on these beliefs to express understandings that suggest ways of establishing and maintaining an effective learning environment

- translate these understandings into classroom practice

- evaluate the practices, identifying effective ones and modifying or changing those that prove less effective.

Cambourne's Natural Learning Model, which we discussed in detail in the previous chapter, is the basis for our entire classroom program.

Physical environment

One of the more important features to consider in setting up a stimulating and effective learning environment is its physical aspect. Some of the elements in the physical environment which deserve careful thought are these.

Print resources — the teacher needs to flood the room with meaningful print, e.g. books, magazines, newspapers, dictionaries, wall print (including charts, maps, displays of children's work, labels, instructions), mobiles, food packets, alphabet cards, number cards, flashcards (including months, days, colours). Children should be involved in the preparation and display of print whenever possible and should use it every day.

Audio-visual resources — e.g. tape recorder, overhead projector, listening post, computer, TV and video.

Variety of writing materials — e.g. small chalkboards, chalk, paper (various colours, sizes, thicknesses), pens, pencils and crayons; computer.

Space organisation — furniture should be arranged to allow flexibility between whole class focuses, group work and individual tasks.

Talking — listening — reading — writing

Whole class focuses

Whole class focuses are times when all of the children are drawn together for a special purpose. They are of course very important when they are used for planned demonstrations, but they are also a necessary organisational feature. At the start of each language session they are used to help settle children down and tune them in to the tasks ahead. They are also times for sharing, for reading to children and for discussing books and language and learning generally.

Co-operative learning (flexible grouping, peer tutoring)

Children tend to learn best when working in small groups. Here they learn easily from one another, partly because they speak a common tongue and share the same mental wavelengths. They also learn from one another because they are bonded in ways that adults can't duplicate. Often they can help each other with a problem because of their own experience with that problem. For instance, Adrian, aged 7, explained where to put the full stop: 'You read it aloud and when you have to take a deep breath, you put the full stop.' It was amazing how many children gained more understanding of punctuation from Adrian's explanation.

We feel that co-operative learning occurs best in small groups of five or six children of mixed ability. Group activities should be designed around general needs and promote discussion, reading and writing. Some should also require children to justify or explain their opinions. Small co-operative learning groups can be excellent examples of the power of peer tutoring and demonstration.

Conferencing

A conference is simply a discussion. It may occur between teacher and child, teacher and children, child and child, or children and children. The purpose of holding a conference is to clarify issues and help children make informed decisions to solve problems and further learning. Conferences are an essential part of whole language classrooms and can provide valuable information to the teacher about each child's abilities and progress in reading and writing, as well as the talking and listening skills manifested in the conference itself.

We have found that the most effective way to conference is on the move. We hit base with each child daily and conferences generally last no longer than 1½ minutes — just long enough to provide immediate help or support, to ask a probing question, to look for justification or clarification of an idea, etc. We do not favour one-to-one conferences lasting 5-10 minutes which mean that children need to book a time to meet with the teacher. Most primary children can be helped very quickly if teachers ensure that they make contact with each child daily, however briefly. And of course a special time (perhaps lunch or recess) can be found for any unusually long piece of writing.

Conferences can be used for many purposes, and some of the following examples reflect the child's point of view, some the teacher's:

- sharing, generating or confirming ideas
- getting opinions on writing in progress
- getting help with writer's block

Collaborative and co-operative learning are vital components of an effective whole language classroom.

- getting reactions
- teaching a point
- introducing a new concept
- developing confidence, critical thinking, active listening
- improving proofreading and editing skills
- focusing children's intentions
- developing awareness of audience
- evaluation
- making children aware of the teacher's presence
- demonstration
- giving praise and support.

In conferencing it is vital to remain positive and constructive to avoid damaging fragile egos. Teachers who speak with each child daily will readily know each child's strengths and weaknesses. They will know when to accept a child's attempts in writing and when to say, 'I think you can do better — let's look at this more closely.' The key to successful conferencing is knowing each child well.

For more information on conferencing, read Jan Turbill's *Now, We Want to Write!* (PETA 1983).

Planned sharing sessions

Leave kids to their own devices and the one thing you can be sure they will do is talk. The talk might range over what they saw on TV, the argument they had in the playground, the way their parents don't understand them. What they are doing is sharing experiences, an activity which comes naturally to language users of all ages.

In a classroom this natural tendency can be turned to advantage and built into the daily activities. Children in a safe, non-threatening environment will gain great benefit from:

- sharing problems they are having with their writing
- sharing the euphoria experienced when they know they have written a piece which required a lot of work and which turned out well
- sharing a loved book with an appreciative audience.

Of course, many of these moments are shared one-to-one or in small group conferences. But sharing with the whole class is a different experience. Because the size of the class necessarily makes the occasion more formal than a small group sharing, children will come to realise the need for a silent rehearsal before the actual session, the importance of having pages marked if they are going to read from a book — the sort of preparation which stops the larger audience from getting bored or tuning out.

Individual reading (DEAR/SSR)

All children need time every day to engage quietly with text, without interruption. It's especially important for immature readers. This time is often called SSR (Sustained Silent Reading). However, very young readers may need to vocalise when reading; they often talk to themselves as they follow the story in text and pictures. So asking them to read in silence would not only be unrealistic but would probably hamper their understanding of the text too. It's better to let this time be a DEAR (Drop Everything And Read) session.

When children mature as readers, however, SSR becomes a much more viable option. It is a time for children to sit by themselves and read a book (or books) without interruption or discussion — this must be saved until the end of SSR. Our feeling is that children need at least one such period a day to engage silently with print, so that they can better interpret what has been written. While we are the first to support discussion as a means of understanding, we also recognise that there are times when everyone needs to reflect and draw conclusions privately.

During SSR we also read silently, demonstrating that we value the experience too. We generally choose children's books — a further demonstration, which helps us keep abreast of the children's reading as well.

Individual writing

Children need to be given time for individual writing every day, and they need opportunities for free choice in writing. Yet they also need direction and exposure to a range of genres, because the greater the exposure they have, the more control of language they can develop.

Free choice of topic will feature more in classrooms where children are *learning to write*, while writing on a set topic will feature more in classrooms where children are *writing to learn*.

When younger children are learning to write, there is a major focus on individual writing in the language session itself. However, when older children are writing to learn, there can be a major focus on individual writing in any of the curriculum areas. Thus they need to be able to write in a variety of genres, selecting the one most appropriate to the work they are doing in a particular area.

There is no prescribed sequence through which every piece of writing must pass. Children will sometimes elect to work on a piece for a considerable period, while at other times they will be satisfied with a first draft. A sensitive teacher will know whether to accept this or to suggest further work.

Planned and unplanned learning

Whole language classrooms have sometimes been represented as rather ad hoc affairs — laissez-faire places where 'anything goes'. Such misunderstandings must derive from classrooms where there is no understanding of the philosophy upon which whole language is based.

In good whole language classrooms there are teachers who program carefully in response to the needs of their children. They structure the language session so that each day children have the opportunity to work both co-operatively and individually, and, while completing the same general task, can work at their own level. They ensure that children are given daily demonstrations of the skills required by competent language users. They take care to provide children with meaningful activities which involve them in using language in order to learn about language. The timetable is predictable, with well-understood routines and ground rules.

Far from being laissez-faire rooms, good whole language classrooms are based on planned learning experiences which suit the range of the children's needs. However, while planning is essential, teachers also need to be constantly alert to the opportunities which arrive throughout the course of every day when they can draw children's attention to a feature of the language they had not planned for. These 'golden moments' of teaching have a lot of impact, for the relevance of the demonstrations which often grow out of them is of real importance to the learner.

Planned demonstrations

Planned demonstrations are an integral feature of a successful whole language classroom. Through them a teacher communicates the know-how of competent language use. They need to be planned so that collectively they meet the general needs of the children and realise the expectations that the teacher holds of them.

We have found the following categories a useful guide when we are planning demonstrations:

- conventions of written language (e.g. spelling, punctuation, sentence structure)
- reading process (e.g. sound/symbol relationships, predicting/confirming)
- writing process (from brainstorming to publishing)
- genre (e.g. recount, narrative, report).

Social environment

Children learn best in a happy, comfortable situation — much like the one in which they learned to talk. They also learn more effectively when they can interact freely and with purpose. An ethos of 'everyone here is a learner' is very comforting and liberating. Teachers who can provide a working atmosphere like this are maximising the opportunities for learning. It needs, of course, effective programming and organisation. Lots of positive teacher-talk and an understanding that support is always available are vital too.

CASE STUDY: KINDERGARTEN

Vonne Mathie

I teach one of four Kindergarten classes in a large primary school (K-6) with over 600 pupils, of whom the greater percentage come from an Anglo-Saxon background. A significant number are of Aboriginal descent, which entitles the school to a Support Teacher - Aboriginal (Learning Difficulties) position and an Aboriginal Education Assistant position. Because of the low socio-economic nature of the community the school receives additional funding through the Disadvantaged Schools Program.

There are sixteen boys and fourteen girls in my class, and at the beginning of the year their ages ranged between 4 years 6 months and 5 years 10 months. These children cover a wide range of ability, maturity and self-confidence, and the quality of their language experience outside the classroom varies considerably.

I endeavour to create and maintain a stimulating, supportive and caring environment where each and every child has the opportunity to participate in effective learning experiences. By this I mean that children:

- are engaged in purposeful activities
- are challenged to think and create
- realise that success is a possibility for everyone

- not only experience the joy of success, but see that success celebrated by the other members of the class family

- come to understand that making mistakes is a natural part of learning and feel secure enough to experiment without fear of criticism

- know they can learn from others and that others can learn from them

- develop their skills and attitudes so that they come to love and value language

- are aware of teacher expectations and realise they have a responsibility to meet them

- accept more and more responsibility for their learning and so become more and more independent as learners

- are familiar with the ground rules of the classroom and try to observe them.

The daily language session

Two hours is the time required for my daily language session. However, the school timetable does not always permit the session to be taken as a two-hour block with an uninterrupted flow from one component to another. On some days it is necessary to accommodate other grade or school activities (e.g. Learning through Play program, Scripture, Assembly) and the language components are then spread over a longer period of the day.

Language learning occurs in classrooms all day, every day. However, for the young Kindergarten child who is just beginning to learn to read and write, I believe it is necessary to include in the language session specific times when I focus on reading and others when I focus on writing.

I also plan language learning activities in other curriculum areas. These provide the child with further opportunities to learn to read or write *or* with opportunities to write or read in order to learn.

The main components of my daily language session are shown in the chart overleaf, and I will now elaborate on each one separately, highlighting its rationale, organisation, implementation and content.

Initial Whole Class Focus

The Initial Whole Class Focus is of vital importance because it is primarily a time of demonstration for language learning. Whether the main focus is on reading or writing, the children are immersed in demonstrations of what print does, how it works, how it is used and what forms it takes. The learning which occurs during these demonstrations can be later translated into practice as the children engage in reading or writing. Thus, for example, Big Book vocabulary which featured in the shared reading segment may later be used by a child composing text during the writing session.

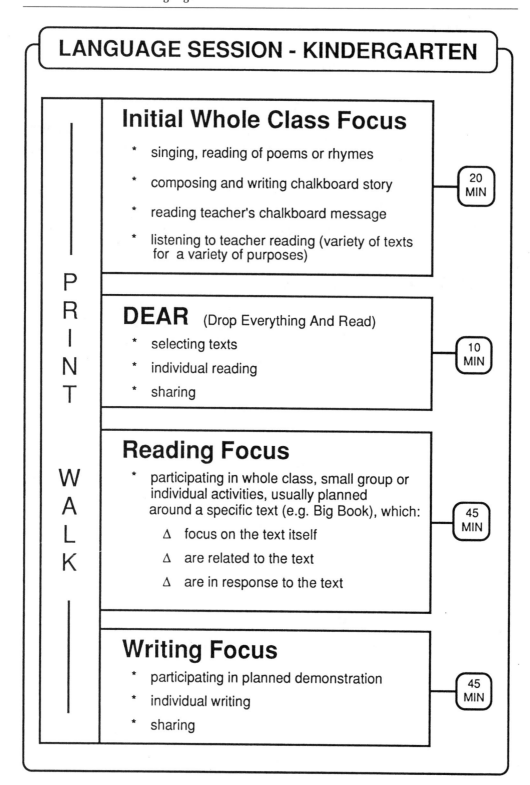

LANGUAGE SESSION - KINDERGARTEN

P R I N T   **W A L K**

Initial Whole Class Focus

* * singing, reading of poems or rhymes
* * composing and writing chalkboard story
* * reading teacher's chalkboard message
* * listening to teacher reading (variety of texts for a variety of purposes)

20 MIN

DEAR   (Drop Everything And Read)

* * selecting texts
* * individual reading
* * sharing

10 MIN

Reading Focus

* * participating in whole class, small group or individual activities, usually planned around a specific text (e.g. Big Book), which:
  * Δ focus on the text itself
  * Δ are related to the text
  * Δ are in response to the text

45 MIN

Writing Focus

* * participating in planned demonstration
* * individual writing
* * sharing

45 MIN

The children always gather on the carpeted area at the front of the room, either facing the chalkboard or the easel. Being seated together in this class group creates a special atmosphere and fosters a feeling of oneness and security as the children support each other in the learning process. It also enables them to see clearly and hear easily, which helps them concentrate. In addition, because I value eye contact when I am telling or reading a story, I find it best to have the children seated together close to me.

While the children gather on the carpet at the beginning of the day, I involve them in the singing of known songs or the reciting of known poems. Children enjoy this type of activity and it also gives me another opportunity to immerse them in print: all the songs and poems are available on charts or overhead transparencies, and I encourage the children to follow the text as we sing or recite.

With the children settled on the carpet, we move on to composing and writing the chalkboard story about the day and weather, which provides an effective modelled writing/reading demonstration. The text usually follows this pattern:

Today is (Monday).	*or*	Today is (Thursday).
It's a (warm), (sunny) day.		It's (cold) today!

The children discuss and decide upon the text for the day, which is then written on a previously ruled section of the chalkboard. At the beginning of the year I usually have to do much of the scribing myself. However, as the children gain more and more control of language, they are more and more able to take over the role of demonstrator — and a demonstration is often more powerful when it's provided by a peer. Most children volunteer enthusiastically to assist with the demonstration (volunteering is necessary if a non-threatening environment is to be maintained). As the various volunteers write the text on the chalkboard, the other children help by suggesting, for example, where certain words may be found, or by commenting on what is written and how it is written. The children read the completed text together and decide whether it makes sense or not. The appropriate punctuation is then added.

Next I write a message on the chalkboard myself. This usually refers to a relevant past, present or future happening, e.g:

We are having our photographs taken today. Smile!

I write the message up without comment. The children are asked to watch this demonstration in silence, although they often find it difficult, especially if words in the text suddenly become meaningful. When I have finished writing, the children are invited to offer suggestions about the meaning of any words in the message. The importance of this stage is that it gives the children an opportunity to discuss and use the cueing systems in a non-threatening situation to bring meaning to the text in front of them. They regard the message as a puzzle to be solved, and when the solution is finally achieved, their excitement and satisfaction are quite evident.

Now it is time for me to read to the children. Although I believe that texts written in a simplified way and with restricted vocabulary (such as many Big Books) have a useful place in the class reading program, I also believe it is essential that even the youngest children are given a number of opportunities each day to interact with normal books. Children learning to read can only have this interaction if the teacher provides time throughout the day for them to listen as he or she reads aloud. It is through special times like these that children develop that all-important love of books and reading — so necessary if they are to become confident and competent readers, who view reading as a purposeful and enjoyable experience.

I always try to read to the children a variety of texts, written for a variety of purposes. My reasons for selecting a particular text to read at this point vary greatly. Maybe it's related to the current Big Book, or to work in another curriculum area. Maybe it demonstrates a specific feature of the writing process, or helps us 'follow' an author. Or maybe it's simply a book which one of the children has brought from home.

I have found that reading to the children towards the end of the Initial Whole Class Focus, just before DEAR time, usually puts them into an enthusiastic frame of mind so that they are keen to select their own texts for the individual reading session that follows.

DEAR (Drop Everything And Read)

I call this component DEAR rather than SSR because in my experience Kindergarten children usually need to vocalise when reading and so silence is not a realistic expectation. None the less even very young children learning to read need to be given time each day to sit down alone with a book of their own choosing, challenged to bring meaning to the text it contains.

A variety of texts must be readily available for the children to select from, e.g. magazines, class library books, school library books, teacher's own library, books related to the Big Book, books related to the current unit of work in another curriculum area, the children's own books.

Within my Kindergarten classroom a routine for DEAR time is established by ensuring that the children understand and abide by some basic rules. At the beginning of the year we have to discuss these rules at the start of each DEAR session. However, as the weeks pass by, the children accept the routine and reference to the rules becomes incidental. Here they are:

- Select two texts. (I encourage the children to choose one familiar text, e.g. a small book version of a Big Book, and another according to their own interest.)

- Return to your own seat, put your books on the desk and fold your arms to let me know you are ready to begin reading. (While some children take extra time to choose, I question the other children about the titles of their books and maybe the reasons for their selection.)

- When everyone is seated, we begin to read quietly (including Miss Mathie).

- During this quiet reading time, everyone stays seated.

DEAR is a time when children begin to discover the joy and satisfaction that reading can give.

- We share *after* individual reading time, *not* during.

After five or ten minutes I suggest to the children that they might like to move to another area in the room to share their texts with a friend. I sometimes round off the session by sharing my text with the children if I want to demonstrate a particular point (e.g. using an index when specific information is required).

The children are then asked to return their books to the appropriate shelves if they do not intend to read them again during the language session.

Reading Focus

During the Reading Focus the children are involved in activities which have been planned around a specific text, e.g. a Big Book. Some of these activities may *focus on the text itself*, e.g. shared reading, cloze, oral retelling, sequencing, spelling strategies, use of speechmarks, vocabulary.

Other activities may be *related to the text* e.g. letter focus. Knowledge of the twenty-six letters of the alphabet and the forty-eight sounds they make is essential if children are to become competent writers and readers. In my classroom there is some separate emphasis on the individual letter names and shapes, but the letter sounds are only treated within the context of a word or sentence. For instance, the children may discuss words like 'apple, aeroplane, apricot, Australia' which all begin with the same letter but differ in initial sound.

Each week I plan activities where the children focus on a particular letter of the alphabet, usually one featured in or associated with the Big Book. Examples of these activities are:

- composing and writing text to suit magazine pictures which have been pasted into a booklet devoted to the featured letter, e.g. 'The Kk Book'
- completing a stencil which requires the children to identify words beginning with the featured letter and eliminate those that don't (there are picture clues to help)
- looking for words beginning with the featured letter within the classroom environment
- using a handwriting stencil to practise the correct lower case formation of the featured letter
- playing with language, e.g. reciting rhymes or tongue twisters
- discussing how the featured letter is shown in the various picture dictionaries within the classroom
- brainstorming words for the featured letter and writing these into a large class dictionary.

Further activities may be *in response to the text* and extend the children's language learning into other curriculum areas, e.g. music, drama, visual arts, health studies, mathematics, science, social studies.

Writing Focus

Although the order may vary to suit particular needs, the Writing Focus always features a planned demonstration, an individual writing session and a sharing session.

Planned demonstration

Planned demonstrations for writing can occur throughout the daily two-hour language session. For example, in the Initial Whole Class Focus I might read a text to highlight character description, or in the Reading Focus I might talk about the use of speech bubbles in a shared book. However, I always include a planned writing demonstration

Liam Apps has brought the name label from his desk to help a friend scribing a text about his birthday. Children readily engage in demonstrations provided by their peers.

within the Writing Focus itself. Sometimes I might read to the children or assume the role of storyteller, but normally I use the modelled writing strategy. The text composed during this session is written (and sometimes illustrated) in a large book of blank pages which is clipped to the easel. This ensures that the children can refer to it later whenever they need to.

The Whole Class Focus structure is usually used for this planned demonstration. However, sometimes I divide the class into groups (e.g. five — one for each day of the week), providing a demonstration for a specific need for one group only each day. This type of organisation does provide greater opportunity for each group member to participate and contribute, though I must again emphasise the importance of including in each group children who cover a wide range of language development.

The purpose of the planned demonstrations is to construct the type of scaffolding that will provide the support young writers need as they attempt to express their thoughts and feelings on paper. Children are often partly aware of their own needs, and they are more likely to engage with a demonstration (and so learn from it) if they sense that it will help them.

Individual writing

In the individual writing session I aim to develop a community of young writers, sometimes working collaboratively, sometimes co-operatively and sometimes alone, but always working to achieve a specific goal each has set.

For me this is above all a time when *children write*, and I have two expectations. Firstly, I expect children to attempt to express their ideas and feelings using *text* (illustrations are optional). Secondly, I expect the children themselves to write that text on their writing paper — I do not scribe for them. Children are challenged by my expectations to accept responsibility for recording their own ideas and feelings, and so I have to ensure that these expectations are realistic. I must know the children well enough to allow for their individual differences, and I must give them the sort of learning environment that supports and encourages their independence.

During individual writing time the children are given many opportunities to exercise freedom of choice. They can choose their own topic, creating their own text from their individual and combined experiences, and so work on tasks which have relevance and meaning for them. They are free to select and use any resources within the learning environment which they consider appropriate, and they are free to choose their working space within the room. To work alone or collaborate with a classmate is also left to individual choice.

There is continual talk during the writing session as children share ideas, seek or provide help, discuss problems and celebrate successes. I am constantly circulating in the room, moving in and out of a variety of roles (consultant, friend, counsellor, teacher, facilitator, learner, researcher) to respond to a variety of needs.

When children have completed their piece of writing for the day, they may choose another language activity, e.g. author's circle, print walk, word games with cards, reading a book, sequencing activity, sharing a book with a friend, listening to a story at the listening post.

Sharing

At the end of each Writing Focus the class gathers in a circle on the carpeted area at the front of the room and the children are given the opportunity to share their writing (or to listen as others share). Pieces of writing which display special achievement or effort are discussed, and their authors are praised and applauded.

Afterwards the children put their sheets of writing in their personal folders, which are stored in plastic tubs — one for each group of tables.

Print Walk

A number of references have already been made to the importance of creating and maintaining a stimulating, meaningful and supportive print environment in the classroom, with as much input from the children as possible. Colourful displays of children's art work with appropriate text help create a stimulating environment.

Equally, involving children in the composing and writing of classroom print helps ensure a meaningful environment, while adding to it in response to children's needs helps maintain a supportive environment. It's also important to retain the print as a support, and so, after removing a display from the wall, I make it available as a class book.

To gain maximum benefit from the print environment children need to use it every day, and here I find the terms *print walk* and *print 'walk'* helpful. A *print walk* is a walk around the room to read various texts on display, while a *print 'walk'* refers to other occasions when the children use only one or two items of classroom print (e.g. following the text as we sing a song).

I try to provide a learning environment where the children are immersed in print by setting up my classroom with the following items:

- *wall displays*, e.g. for the colours - a garden of flowers; for the months - the Birthday Train; for the buses which carry us to and from school - a large bus packed with self-portraits; for the days of the week - 'Bananas in Pyjamas' song; for a Big Book wall story - art work with supporting text in sequential order

- *charts*, e.g. nursery rhymes, innovations on Big Book texts, songs, class rules, recipes, instructions how to ...

- *suspended displays* (hung from flex stretched across the room), e.g. underwater scene (fish, seaweed) with the rhyme, 'One, two, three, four, five,/Once I caught a fish alive ... '

- *mobiles*, e.g. 'The Enormous Watermelon' with appropriate vocabulary attached on leaves

- *sets of flashcards* which match texts on display, e.g. months, days, colours, numbers, body parts, family members

- *commercial cards*, e.g. alphabet letters, numbers 1-10 and 1-24, shapes, rhymes

- *complete alphabet cards* for individual use

- *labels*, e.g. name labels and alphabet and number strips on desks; elsewhere other labels such as, 'This is where we keep our writing folders' or 'We love books!'

- *books*, e.g. school library books (bulk loan), class library books (changed each term), my own library, Big Book packs, children's own books

- *individual word-bank boxes* i.e. takeaway food containers (if a child needs a word which cannot be found in the classroom environment, I print that word on a card to be kept in his or her word bank)

- *songs and rhymes* on overhead transparencies and on cards (these are put in plastic pockets and stored in a folder, and the children enjoy using them during individual writing time).

Within my classroom there are also special areas for special purposes, e.g. listening post, mathematics display shelf, construction toy display shelf, dolls' corner, class shop — 'The Purple Pantry'.

A typical day — putting it all together

Friday - Week 10 - Term 3

The thirty children in my class hang their school bags outside and wander into the room. Some seat themselves immediately on the carpet, while others go the the 'special box' and put in any important item they have brought for a sharing session (news) later in the day. While the slower ones get themselves ready, I turn on the cassette recorder and play the accompaniment for this week's new song, 'Let's Go Fly a Kite'. As the children sing the song, I encourage them to follow as I point our way through the text on the overhead. (Sometimes one of the children does the pointing.)

When we are all assembled and I have dealt with some routine matters (absence notes, excursion money), we recite 'The Wriggle Rhyme'. Then we turn our attention to the chalkboard story. We discuss the day and the weather and agree on the following text:

> Today is Friday. It's a warm, sunny day.

One by one children volunteer to assist with the scribing of this text until it's finished. They use a variety of spelling strategies (e.g. copying environmental print, memory, letter sounds). After reading it through, they wait expectantly for me to write up today's special message:

> We are very excited today because our school fete will open at twelve o'clock. Hooray!

After much discussion, the mystery of the language puzzle is finally solved and the children enthusiastically read through the message together.

They now gather around my chair near the easel to listen as I read Ruth Park's story, *When the Wind Changed*. Before I read, we discuss the cover, title, author and illustrator (Deborah Niland). I invite the children to make predictions about the story plot and then begin to read. Sometimes I pause to ask a question, to seek comment, to clarify, or to encourage predictions. When I have finished, I ask the children to make personal comments about the story. I now turn back to the beginning of the book and start to turn the pages, encouraging the children to retell the story as we move from one illustration to the next.

It's now DEAR time. The children move around the room to select the two texts they will read by themselves. When they have made their choice, they go to their desks and sit down to wait until everyone is ready to begin reading. Today the pause is long enough for me to ask a few of them if they will say a little about the books they have chosen and why. Once reading begins I encourage all of them to be as quiet as possible, though most need to verbalise as they read. I also read at this time

— today I'm reading a recipe book which was brought in for one of our cooking sessions this week.

After about ten minutes I am aware that most children are ready to share a book with a friend. I announce that they may now join a friend anywhere within the room and I encourage them to read a book (or a section of a book) to that friend. I close the session by asking the children to put back their books unless they think they will need to refer to them again later (especially during the writing session).

The children now move back onto the carpeted area in front of the easel for a shared reading of our Big Book, *Woosh!*. Just before we start, the children turn to greet one of our parents who has arrived to assist with an activity group. We turn our attention back to the text and enjoy the story together.

After the shared reading session the children break up into three groups. Children doing Activity 3 move quietly to their task area. Half of them sit at the listening post and prepare to follow the story *Bounce*. The others sit at a nearby group of tables to complete the 'Kk' letter stencil.

Children doing Activity 2 move excitedly to their task area, where our parent will help them construct their own kites, which they will later take into the playground to fly.

Children doing Activity 1 remain with me on the floor near the easel, where we will innovate on *Woosh!* and then paint illustrations to support the new text. Today we also have to devise an appropriate ending for the previous days' innovations!

The group activities continue for about forty minutes, after which the children assemble again on the carpeted area at the front of the room. One child from each group reports on today's activities, and we thank our parent for her assistance with the kite activity during the week.

For the next five minutes the children and I go on a print walk round the room to read text from displays, charts and mobiles. We then gather at the front of the room for another whole class focus — this time a writing demonstration.

There is much excitement in the class today because of the school fete and I have previously decided to make it the topic for today's modelled writing. I start a discussion about the fun events we know have been organised for the afternoon — things to buy, games to play and displays to watch and enjoy. We decide to list the main points of our discussion on the chalkboard. Sometimes I write a word — always 'thinking aloud' as I write the letters to demonstrate a specific spelling strategy — and sometimes children volunteer to write a word. Those who do are praised for their efforts; applause is often spontaneous! The lower section of the chalkboard is soon covered with print and attention shifts to the large class writing book which is attached to the easel. I write today's date in the top right-hand corner and my name in the left. I tell the children that today I want my text to be about how I am going to spend my time and money at the fete. During the next ten minutes I encourage all of them to participate by contributing ideas, composing text, suggesting appropriate spelling strategies and scribing. Then we read through the text to check whether it makes sense. When we are completely satisfied with the meaning, we leave our class story and begin discussing individual writing time.

The children are eager to start on their own writing and move to their desks. The computer paper is quickly distributed and they all write down their names and the date. Some children choose to remain and work at their own desks, while others move to sit with a classmate or to one of the carpeted areas around the room.

As the children begin to put their thoughts on paper, it is interesting to observe their topic choices: some are writing about the fete (either copying the class story or describing their own anticipations of the coming afternoon); others are concentrating on ideas which have no connection with the fete whatsoever.

Because we have been experiencing writing sessions for several months now, the children know that illustrations are optional and that I expect them to use text to express their ideas on paper. Some children are illustrating first and will then label their illustrations; others are intent upon composing several sentences of text. However, none of them expects me to scribe for them: they have accepted that composing and writing the text is their responsibility. At the beginning of the year I deliberately refused to scribe for them, continually encouraging them to do so for themselves because it was vital for their learning to convey my expectations to them: 'You can do it! I'm here to help you, but you must try for yourself.' Consequently they are developing many coping strategies to assist them with the writing process.

There is a buzz of conversation in the room as children share their ideas, seek advice and offer assistance to one another.

Jillian helps Kristy as she tries to spell a word using symbol/sound relationships.

Scott and Sandra read the book *Grandpa Grandpa* together, searching for the word 'fishing' in the text.

Cheryl copies 'treasure sticks' from the chalkboard.

Steven and Craig search the song folder for 'teddy bears'.

Mathew and Casey are spreading out the cards from Mathew's word-bank box, trying to identify the word 'tree'.

Heidi is sharing her story about the pillow fight event at the fete with David. They laugh together over the illustration.

Michael is asking Graham, a confident writer, to help him with the spelling of a word.

I circulate in the room, always on the move, seeking to identify and respond to the needs of individual children. I find myself *encouraging* a child to continue with an idea; *advising* how to overcome writer's block; *praising* effort (especially a young learner's attempts to control language, i.e. approximations); *expressing disappointment* over minimum effort; *suggesting* collaboration on a particular problem (or working alone if collaboration seems not to be helping); *listening* to children who want to share their achievements or to children who are frustrated by their efforts; *questioning* so that I can help children solve problems for themselves, or so that I can find out more about what they have learnt and how they have learnt it.

Thus my role is ever changing as I move in and out of a variety of situations which call on me to become in turn a —

consultant: Emma is uncertain about the length of her piece and asks me to comment.

friend: Bradley is excited about what he has written. I sit down to listen as he reads his description of gumboot throwing.

counsellor: Jonathan is frustrated by his attempts, screws up his paper and throws it onto the floor. I move over to him with another piece of paper. Talking quietly, I question him to identify his problem. I suggest that I am willing to work with him for a while. He eventually picks up his pencil and writes his name on the second sheet of paper. Together we find the word he needs from the chalkboard list. He writes it on his paper and is now happy to continue to work alone.

teacher: Graham asks me to demonstrate how to form an omission mark because he needs another word in his text for the meaning to be clear.

facilitator: Various children ask for help with spelling. My response differs according to my expectations for each particular child, e.g:

'Let's see if we can find it on this chart'.

'Why don't you ask Sam about that word? I'm sure he knows how to spell it.'

'I'd like you to have a go yourself. Listen to the sounds and see if you can write down letters for each sound you can hear. Come back after you've tried and we'll talk about what you've done'.

'I don't think we would find that word amongst the room print, so watch me as I write it for you on a card. Then you can copy it from there and store it in your word bank.

researcher: I spend a lot of time talking with the children, and in particular I question them about their learning — 'Why did you write that?' 'How did you know that?' Their answers help me to discover more about the learning process and help them to focus on what they've done, so that they can better realise their new knowledge and transfer it to other situations. I also take time to stand back and observe the behaviour of these young learners, making a mental note of what I see. Later in the day I will reflect on these times of interaction and observation and write onto the children's anecdotal record cards, and into my journal, important discoveries for the day. These entries form an important part of my assessment/evaluation records.

As children complete their piece of writing for the day, they move on to another language activity, e.g. author's circle, print walk, reading a favourite book alone or with a friend, or listening to a story at the listening post.

There are some children who would be quite happy to continue writing all day, but I decide to bring the session to a close because most of them are now involved

Sequencing the text of a favourite song is another language activity children can choose when they have finished writing.

in other activities. I ask the children to bring their pieces of writing to share in a circle and call for volunteers. Most are keen to share, but some prefer to listen. As a variety of texts are shared, I use them to demonstrate specific points about the language learning process.

There is a knock at the door. A Year 6 child announces that the parachute jumpers from the nearby Naval Base will soon be landing in the playground. The children begin to chatter excitedly amongst themselves as they stow today's writing in their folders and gather at the door. This imminent happening will probably be a popular topic in our next writing session!

CASE STUDY: YEAR 4

Hazel Brown

I work in a school in which all classes are paralleled in terms of academic ability. Accordingly the children in my class range from two who are just beginning to read and write to three or four who already have excellent control of a wide range of language processes and skills. Three children come from families where a second language is spoken at home.

Each child in this class needs individual attention and care; each child needs support and encouragement; each child needs to feel and be an achiever and to have this acknowledged; each child needs challenge. Here's how I cater for the needs of my Year 4 children.

Expectations

Expectations (often referred to as objectives) need to be determined first. Mine are initially very general but give me direction. As I later program units of work they become more detailed with regard to the skills and processes I want to promote, supplying the guidelines by which I evaluate language control. My expectations take account of developing the attitudes, understanding the processes and controlling the skills needed by literate people, and they include:

- positive attitudes towards learning
- seeking/accepting advice willingly
- accepting responsibility for learning and organisation
- accepting mistakes as a natural part of learning
- having the confidence to discuss learning
- accepting the need for justifications in discussion and argument
- control of a variety of genres in reading, writing and speaking
- making considered decisions about reading, writing and speaking
- understanding the need for preparedness/correctness when going public
- consulting a variety of sources in search of information
- reading for a sustained period of time
- recognising good/bad miscues
- having strategies to overcome blocks in reading and writing
- understanding the value of re-reading for information
- making a positive attempt to edit
- displaying a developing vocabulary

- controlling the conventions of writing

- understanding the elements of various forms of writing

- applying knowledge.

Physical environment

My classroom is presently in a fairly new block. It is carpeted, with a wet, or work area, and a small study room shared with the adjoining class off to one side. The furniture is arranged so that it accommodates our needs — floor space, work tables and isolated work areas to suit both individuals and small groups.

There are large bookshelves along two walls. On these I have separated fiction from non-fiction and labelled accordingly. On the non-fiction and reference shelves are:

- complete set of junior encyclopedia (with index)

- 12 dictionaries (assorted)

- 2 thesauruses

- 6 word books

- 15 atlases (assorted)

- bulk loan books from library (approx. 80 on current theme)

- assorted non-fiction books from library, chosen by children at start of term to keep in room (20)

- magazines (various)

- telephone directories

- my own books, either bought, donated or salvaged, or ones my own children have grown out of.

On the shelves labelled fiction, books are arranged in the following categories:

- picture books (15)

- by author — children like to read lots of books by the same author once they have acquired a 'taste' (50)

- poetry books (12)

- books of plays (10)

- fiction books ranging from those with lots of pictures and little text, e.g. *Thing*, to longer, continuous text with few pictures, e.g. *The Haunting* (200).

While many of these books are my own, a large number come from the school library. I take my class to the library once or twice a term and tell them to choose two books each that they would like to have in our classroom. In addition, with our dedicated librarian's help, I also select a range of books which aren't necessarily connected with a theme to have in our room. Librarians are the most underused resource in the school. They know what books children read and enjoy and their

Children should be encouraged to use reference material regularly.

help in selecting books for a classroom should always be sought. Most librarians believe it is better to get books into rooms where they are used than to keep them in libraries gathering dust.

Altogether, then, I have about 300 books in my room — an important part of the concept of immersion. Moreover there is lots of print around the room — on windows, doors, pinboards and mobiles. All of it was made in consultation with the children and so it all has meaning for them. There are:

- pear shapes of homophones above one chalkboard

- pictures from stories with accompanying text on the door

- the *Animalia* frieze with words identifying objects in the pictures under one chalkboard

- large diagrams of insects with accompanying statements on a window

- lists of synonyms for 'nice', 'went' and 'big' under the second chalkboard

- photos of butterflies with explanatory statements on a wall

- mobiles of the stages in the life cycle of the butterfly with statements suspended through them

- 'word pictures', both similes and metaphors, covering another window

- sequence of children's paintings of scenes from *The Iron Man*, with the story written underneath, covering a pinboard in the wet area

- a large mural of 'The Land of Geometrica' (creatures and landscape made from mathematical shapes and labelled) covering a full pinboard, with a range of mathematical words/terms above
- a 'yellow brick road' and pictures of Oz characters on the door to the study room, with retellings of episodes in the story on the walls inside
- on another wall, a large sheet of paper recording the children's opinions on a comparison between book and film versions of *The Wizard of Oz*.

Print in books, print on walls; the physical aspects of immersion.

Organisation

The initial structure needed for a successful program in any classroom is a time and motion plan, a basic organiser for learning activities to ensure that each day children get to engage in the 'features of a whole language classroom' described in the opening section of this chapter. Such a plan must ensure that children will:

- have whole class needs addressed
- have personal and specific needs addressed
- read, write and discuss
- work both individually and co-operatively
- experience planned demonstrations
- experience planned learning times
- make personal choices and decisions
- experience support and challenge
- have ready access to resources.

I am fortunate in having an uninterrupted two-hour block at the beginning of every morning, and this is timetabled as being my major thrust each day in developing language. How I organise this time is set out in the diagram opposite.

What happens when?

Whole class focus

I always start the day with the class as a whole group sitting on the floor in front of my chair. It is a time of settling down and tuning in, and, for a major part of each term, I spend it largely in reading to the children from an ongoing serial. Older children love this sort of continuity. It allows them time to reflect on what has been read and to project onwards and hypothesise about what is to come. It is an intimate time with all participants bonded by the story. It is a time for incredible discussion of author's intent, reader's interpretation, the power of words,

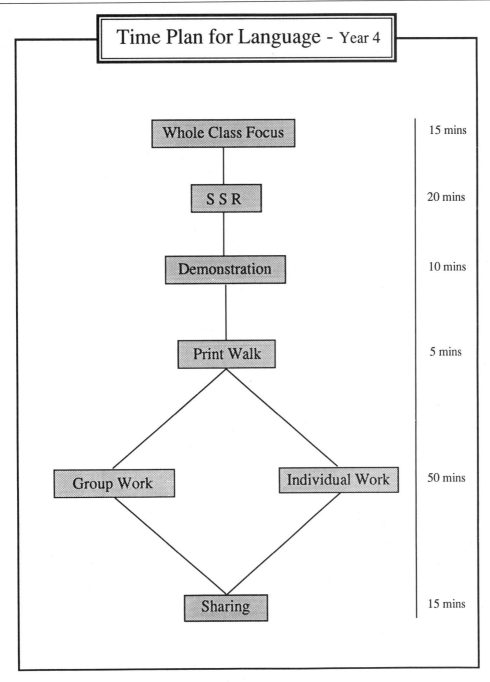

the importance of style, the clarity of description, the value of illustrations. It is not a time for 'How closely did you listen, how well have you understood?' or ten comprehension-type questions to close the chapter. Children need time to let stories seep in, to match what they've heard with their experiences, to move with the tale. And so I read, maybe pausing occasionally for reflection, or to make a personal comment. At the end I always allow a short time for reflection before I promote discussion which will invoke values and opinions and lead children into making judgements about the author's strengths in creating a worthwhile story. The sort of questions I ask don't anticipate a predictable answer:

> 'Did you get a clear picture of the Coorong? How do you think Thiele achieved that?'

Sometimes I vary the serial pattern by sharing a Big Book, or by reading a complete story or book, or a section of a book (e.g. non-fiction, poetry, author profile). Serial reading usually leads into a follow-on activity of varying duration such as:

- story grammar chart (4-5 days)
- literary sociogram (2-3 days)
- plot profile (1-2 days)
- story map (2 days)
- literary countdown (2 days)
- innovations on text.

More information about all these activities except the last can be found in Johnson & Louis (1985). A helpful reference for text innovations is *Story Box* (Rigby).

SSR (Sustained Silent Reading)

This is a time the children really look forward to — it is an engagement I am loath to break and often extends beyond its allotted span. It is a time when children sit by themselves and read silently, without interruption or discussion. This must be saved until the end of SSR. My feeling is that children need at least one such period a day to engage quietly with print. And because quiet is essential when readers are settled, I encourage children to choose a book or books which will keep them occupied for at least 10 minutes. During this period children are not allowed to change books at all. They therefore learn to choose responsibly. Reselecting after this time must be done quietly, without disturbing others.

I like children to sit at their desks to read. Experience has shown that here they are more settled and more comfortable. And although I give settled readers the option of sitting in other places, such as on the cushions, they invariably gravitate back to their desks.

Demonstration

Demonstrations must meet a need, and these needs can easily be determined by teachers who circulate around the room when children are working. If they sit and talk to children, read their work and listen to them read, problems or needs can readily be detected. Demonstrations can then be programmed if the need is seen

Environmental print needs to be used regularly: here the topic of discussion is group badges and emblems.

to be a fairly general one. There is no substitute for being a kid-watcher and an active participant in the learning of language.

The four major areas of language learning where I believe children need demonstrations to develop their language control have already been listed on p. 24. When planning demonstrations I refer to these categories, linking them to my observations of the children.

Whenever I demonstrate to children, regardless of age, I sit them on the floor in front of my chair and the easel. I believe this closeness is necessary for engagement to occur.

Print walk

Rooms which have plenty of stimulating print hung on walls, windows and doors are exciting places to be in. They are a reflection of the learning which is occurring and a stimulus to further learning. The environmental print in my classroom is a valuable resource for the children as it contains ideas and models of writing they can relate to: examples of conventional spelling, grammar, punctuation, layout/format, story starters, descriptive writing, etc. And of course this wealth of words is a much more powerful resource if the children are regularly referred to it before they write.

So, each day just before writing time, I 'walk' my children through one section of our environmental print. We read it and discuss it. It provides a basis for demonstrating such things as spelling patterns, use of speech marks or models for poetry writing. Such continual exposure shows the children that wall print is a useful resource, which I expect them to use as reference material when they write — books are not necessarily the better reference for young children.

Group work

In order to maximise learning, the children in my class take turns to work together once a week in small groups of mixed ability. They work on an activity designed around general needs which requires them to talk to each other — to rationalise, argue, justify and explain — as well as to read or write in order to complete it. The less able have things explained to them in simple terms by those more competent. The bright sparks deepen their understanding by having to order and communicate their thoughts. All children are extended by having to make decisions and justify them.

Each group works at a place conveniently separated from children who are working on their own writing, such as a special work table, floor space or the adjoining study room. The range of activities includes several which sometimes involve the whole class after a serial reading (see p. 44), as well as:

- spelling/word power/vocabulary games
- co-operative cloze
- play or poetry reading
- group story or report
- sequencing activity
- brainstorming activity (e.g. descriptive words for characters in a story I've previously read, to be later made into a game).

Individual work

The time in my class allocated to individual work is structured so that the children experience related reading and writing, often in a genre determined by me — in which case they are contracted to complete a piece of writing in a set number of weeks, usually three.

At the start of the school year I plan the genres which I will focus on that year. (There is a school policy designed to ensure that certain genres are covered by all grades, every year.) This plan provides me with a focus for:

- teacher reading
- planned demonstrations
- bulk loan of library books
- activities for co-operative learning
- individual work.

The way all of this fits together can be seen better in the following section, which describes a typical day in my classroom.

In the 50 minutes allowed for individual work children may be reading, note taking, discussing, writing, conferencing, drawing or publishing. The kind of activity will determine where they work, e.g. desks, work table, floor, group study room, library, computer room.

In addition to the teacher-determined task children may also be involved with:

- free writing
- free reading
- listening post for songs (with wordsheets)
- activities tied to a book which has been read
- general knowledge quiz.

The object of having children work through a weekly general knowledge quiz is to give them a regular and purposeful activity which requires them to use an atlas, dictionary, thesaurus and encyclopedia, so that they not only add to their general knowledge of our world but also develop their ability to use reference material. It is part of a process of moving them to a position where they can use reference material to help solve a problem to which they don't have a ready answer. Knowing how and where to find information is an essential ingredient in becoming literate and learned.

The skills I require of children in completing this quiz are regularly demonstrated in class. Moreover all of the answers are to be found within the room, where the resources include the encyclopedia and the various atlases, dictionaries and thesauruses listed earlier (p. 40).

Having such resources available in the room enables me to watch children using them and to track their development in such things as skim reading, locational skills, alphabetical ordering, reading with understanding, etc. And each area of the quiz is designed to further the knowledge and understanding of something which has already been treated in class, i.e. the questions are not random.

Sharing

Sharing is a very personal experience for the sharer and children therefore need lots of encouragement and support. Each child must come to it in his or her own time. It is a quick-kill action to place all children on a roster for sharing, for there is nothing to gain in forcing a child to share if the experience is traumatic. It is far better to allow confidence to accumulate by encouraging such a child to share with close friends in smaller, more intimate groups. The sensitive teacher will model response here by being positive, encouraging effort and celebrating progress. Children can then select from these examples of response when commenting on another's work. Everyone likes to be acknowledged for effort and product, and positive response tends to snowball, encouraging even the more timid children to share their language work.

Sharing takes place with the whole class grouped in a circle which includes the sharer's chair. Volunteers share one at a time — perhaps a piece of their writing in draft or finished form, perhaps a favourite book or a poem they have learned. They may be seeking help or opinions; they may wish to share their own successes, their insights or simply their delight in good writing.

Synthesis — a typical day

The best way to show how all of this fits togehter is to describe a typical day in my classroom. I have selected a Monday half-way through Term 1 — the second Monday of a four-week program designed to develop the children's skills in report writing. During the previous week I had introduced the topic, 'Insects', modelled the writing of a science report and demonstrated how to read a diagram. We had examined the labelling of several insect diagrams and the children had brought in specimen insects to observe and record. We had surveyed the range of information provided in a selection of books on bees, looking carefully at the chapter headings, subheadings and the relationship between contents page and index. We had also discussed how to categorise information, and the children had begun reading, note taking and summarising.

Now, on the second Monday of the program, we begin with ...

Whole class focus

This session focuses on the use and value of diagrams as a substitute for text in a non-fiction book or report, reinforcing some of last week's work. It involves me in:

- showing the children a diagram of a beehive with labelled sections
- encouraging them to generate information from the diagram, i.e. to 'read it'
- promoting discussion about the value of diagrams and whether or not it's necessary to have accompanying text.

SSR

Many children have chosen from the range of non-fiction books on insects, borrowed from the library. About half continue with a book started in the last few days; two or three are reading picture books and one child has a book without words. I am pleased by the discretion children show in their choices, and by the speed with which 'hush' time develops.

Demonstration

This demonstration of how to construct a written report is a follow-up to a similar one given last week. I begin by telling the children that I have been researching the mosquito and that I have gathered together some interesting information. Then I start to think aloud as I write on a large sheet of butcher's paper pinned to a board.

Hazel Brown begins her mosquito report; note the rich array of children's work on the wall behind her.

'O.K. I'd better begin with a major heading at the top and underline it so that people will know what it's all about.

'Now, I want to let people know that it's a tiny insect which can cause disease, and is found in many countries, especially warm ones. I think I'd better write that in an introduction.'

So I use a subheading, 'Introduction', and construct this part of the text in front of the children. Still thinking aloud, I decide that I should inform people of the life cycle of the mosquito by drawing it as a flow chart. Using another subheading, 'Life Cycle of Mosquito', I draw the different stages, explaining as I go.

Then, because time is up, I stop, leave the half-completed poster on the board and tell the children I will work on it some more tomorrow. This will be the basis of my planned demonstration for two or three days this week.

During this period of thinking aloud I am transmitting my knowledge and understanding of report writing to my class. I am not only constructing meaning, but also demonstrating how to communicate it in a simple, logical and acceptable way, so that other people can share the knowledge.

Print walk

The children and I move across the room to a display of large photographs presenting the life of a butterfly. Each has explanatory statements written underneath. We look at one which shows the various stages in the life cycle of the caterpillar and as a class we read aloud these statements:

> Caterpillars grow quickly.
> As they grow they shed their skin several times.
> These stages of growth are called instars.

I then promote discussion to focus the children's attention on spelling configurations and language characteristics.

> 'What spelling patterns can you see in the print we've just read?' Answers suggest such things as double letters, silent 'e's, compound words, syllables.

> 'How is this language different to story language?' Discussion ranges over the telling of facts, shorter sentences, lack of similes and descriptive language, no plot, etc.

Not only have children been reminded during this short segment of the location of words they might need to use in their writing, but also of other aspects of our whole language puzzle.

Next I ask 'Mondays' group of children to stay on the mat near me. The other children are told to continue working on their insect reports.

Group work

The activity to be completed by each group this week is a joint read and retell of a flow chart, 'The Life Cycle of the Dragonfly'. Each child is given a copy, and this is the substance of my instructions.

- Look at the diagram carefully and decide what each part is telling you.
- Consider why the diagram has arrows and a broken line, and why the shape is circular.
- When you have all had a good look at the diagram individually, I want the group to write it up as a report. You will all help, but one person should be chosen to act as scribe. Solve your own problems, don't come to me.

The task involves the children spending some time initially looking at the diagram and then discussing:

- what it is saying
- where the cycle starts
- who is going to act as scribe
- whether the report is going to be written as a continuous text, in point form, or using a heading and subheadings.

A great deal of learning takes place within the group as the children start to translate their thoughts orally, and as these are either rejected or refined before the accepted composition is written down.

Because the children know I am only asking for a first draft, all their effort goes into creating a logical interpretation of the diagram. If this report is later published, they know they will be called upon to turn it into a standard English form.

When the draft is complete, the scribe reads it back to the group. After one or two changes it is placed in front of my chair. The children then go off to work individually on their general knowledge quiz or their insect reports, to read, play a language game, or write something personal. At a convenient moment before the language session ends, I will call them back together to explain their flow chart interpretations to me.

Individual work

While I have been speaking to the group (7-10 minutes), the other children have been settling into their individual work. Everywhere in the room there are on-task children, using language in order to learn about language and thereby gain more control over language.

Jason is still studying his cockroach in its observation box. He is drawing it, adding labels and writing a general description.

Carmel is reading about the ant community. From a section headed 'Types of Ants' she reads a passage several times, closes the book and retells the information in her work book.

Caroline is finishing *Aranea*, a story she hadn't been able to find in SSR.

Daniel has started to draft his insect report. He has a large heading, 'Butterflies and Moths', and a subheading, 'Introduction'. He is writing about the differences between butterflies and moths and has his notes, taken the previous week from reference books, beside him.

Matthew and Peter are having a discussion (conference) on the floor about how many diagrams Peter can put in his report without spoiling it.

Tanya and Jennifer are working on their general knowledge quiz together. They are indentifying three countries which lie on the Tropic of Capricorn.

Kelly is copying the spelling of 'camouflage' from a wall chart.

I move continually, checking on what children are doing, asking for clarification, offering advice or help, re-focusing them if they get off track, joining in on conferences. I also keep an eye on the co-operative learning group as I pass to check if they are coping. I try to become a participant in all the learning that is occurring — there is no better way to get to know children and their learning behaviours. Occasionally, as I notice something particularly relevant to a certain child, I make a note of it in my Anecdotal Records book.

During this period of individual work children may change their activity once or twice. So I can observe them doing a wide range of activities, switching from passive (reading) to active (conferencing, general knowledge, language games, etc.), or vice versa, as time passes.

Sharing

Twenty minutes before recess I ask children to stop work and move to the sharer's circle. Caroline is chairing the session this morning. She asks for volunteers and selects Matt, who moves to the sharer's chair. He wants help with a piece of writing started prior to our report writing project and introduces it.

'Good morning everyone. Today I would like to share with you a piece of writing that I'm having problems with and I need help. I've already conferenced with Caroline and Daniel but I didn't like their suggestions, so I thought the whole class might have more ideas in helping me to find a better ending for the story I've written. I think I finish it too quickly.'

Matt then reads the story to the circle of his classmates. They listen attentively, and when he's finished they start to question him.

'Do you want a happy ending?'

'Do you think the main character should solve the mystery or will he get help from the adults?'

'Did you think the story out before you started writing or did it just happen as you wrote it?'

'I think ....'

Matt responds to each comment or question until eventually he starts to sort things out in his own mind. He thanks the audience and vacates the chair for the next sharer. Problems like his are not always solved, but sharing does usually help to clarify the issues.

All too quickly we have exhausted two hours and the music plays to signify recess. I feel satisfied that the children have been productive and gained more insight into our language. They leave the room, many still talking enthusiastically about their work this morning.

Chapter Four

ASSESMENT AND EVALUATION

Assessment and evaluation are integral components of the language learning process, vital for identifying both class and individual needs so that relevant learning experiences can be planned and implemented. However, the purpose of this chapter is not to cover all the possibilities for assessment and evaluation, but to share the strategies and procedures that we find useful in our whole language classrooms. Readers who wish to add to the strategies we discuss, or who need a more comprehensive overview, should consult E. Daly (ed.), *Monitoring Children's Language Development* (ARA 1989) and M. Kemp, *Watching Children Read and Write* (Nelson 1987).

What suits us?

Working within a naturalistic/wholistic framework for learning language, we quickly realised that the more traditional, rationalistic methods of assessing language were totally unsuitable. Standardised tests of reading or spelling purport to measure skills, and these only at one point in time. We needed strategies which could help us to build up a store of information about each child's literacy development — something just not possible with mass testing. Because we view literacy development as an ongoing process, we were and are looking for markers or indicators of *change* in:

- *attitudes* towards learning
- understanding of the *processes* which underpin language use
- control of the *skills* necessary for literacy.

Because we are looking at change, one-off tests are useless. Rather we believe that teachers should systematically observe children in the language-using situations they are involved in daily, and also collect and analyse samples of the written work they produce. Of course this kind of assessment means working alongside children so as to know them better, i.e. becoming kidwatchers. Our understandings are summarised in the diagram below.

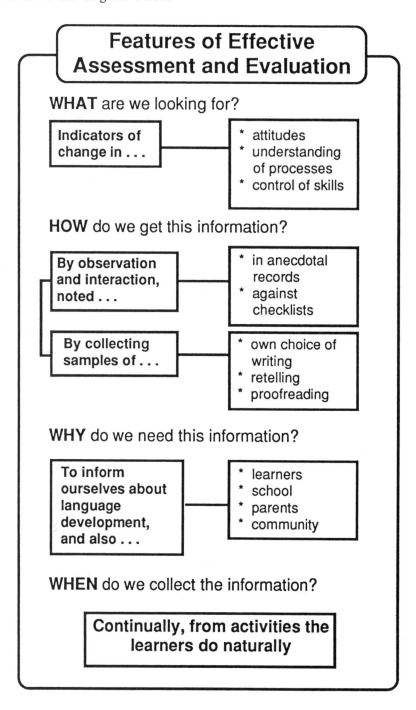

Features of Effective Assessment and Evaluation

WHAT are we looking for?

| Indicators of change in . . . | * attitudes
* understanding of processes
* control of skills |

HOW do we get this information?

| By observation and interaction, noted . . . | * in anecdotal records
* against checklists |

| By collecting samples of . . . | * own choice of writing
* retelling
* proofreading |

WHY do we need this information?

| To inform ourselves about language development, and also . . . | * learners
* school
* parents
* community |

WHEN do we collect the information?

Continually, from activities the learners do naturally

Observation and interaction

Observation and interaction are valuable tools in assessment. They allow the teacher to tap into learning, not only in conferences and sharing sessions, but during any naturally occurring activity in any language-based subject. However, doing this means learning to ask a child the right kind of questions, e.g.

'Tell me, what are you doing?'

'Why are you doing it that way?'

'Have you read anything similar to this before?'

'Why did you decide on ...?'

'Show me how you got this ....'

So, by questioning and observing, the teacher can map progress over time, identifying specific aids to learning, problems the learner encounters and how the problems are resolved. The range of information gathered may cover such areas as:

- attitudes towards learning
- degree of independence/responsibility
- vocabulary
- confidence
- variety of genres attempted
- knowledge of genre characteristics
- length of piece (reading/writing/speaking)
- comprehension of text
- strategies to overcome blocks in reading/writing
- kind of miscues made
- ability to justify/argue logically/be objective/summarise
- editing/proofreading ability
- control of the conventions of standard English.

The salient points of the information collected are written up in anecdotal records. As can be seen from the two specimens we have included overleaf, these don't need to be lengthy or time-consuming. They should simply be a record of what happened — noted down, if possible, as soon as they occur. They can later be reflected upon and interpreted in the light of further information which may make interpretation easier.

Information gained from observation and interaction can also be recorded against checklists of expectations. Such checklists will vary widely according to children's ages, their degree of language control and the language areas covered. What goes into them will also reflect individual teachers' values and understandings about

Name	Graham	
Class	K. Purple	
8/2	Illustration – two people and a dog	
10/2	Copied name – "Graham".	
16/2	Illustrations very detailed – enjoys discussing them with other children and myself.	
17/2	Labelled figures in illustration with "Graham" and "dad".	
23/2→22/3	Detailed illustrations, but no text!	
23/3	Copied text from Big Book, *The Hungry Giant* – " I'll hit you with my bommy – knocker!". Illustration supported text. Read text to me.	
11/4	Wrote full name – "Graham Ian Dean".	
22/4	Labelled illustration with – "That's a (copied environmental print) monster (letter sounds using alphabet card with teacher assistance)." Used a full stop.	
26/4 → 19/5	Illustrations continue to be detailed and Graham is enthusiastic about discussing them, either with individuals or the whole class during sharing time. However, he prefers to be a "safe" writer, only willing to write text where the conventional spelling is available to him. Reluctant to use temporary spelling.	
25/5	Labelled illustration (after much encouragement) with the text – "I (memory) went (letter sounds using alphabet card) to (memory) Green (copied environmental print) Patch (letter sounds using alphabet card with teacher assistance)." Used a full stop.	
8/6	Worked independently – used temporary spelling! Labelled his illustration with the text – "I went to Lona Pac (Luna Park)".	

language learning, because these will determine what expectations they hold of any particular child or group of children.

<u>Caroline</u> (Year 4)

16/2	Quiet, conscientious, co-operative ; appears to enjoy reading /writing
24/2	Shared on "Stuart Little" by E.B. White - clear /confident. Remarked - 'This book is nothing like Charlotte's Web; totally different style. They sound as if they were written by different authors.'
3/4	Wrote 2 buddy class stories - well written and comprehensive. Teaching point was the apostrophe of possession.
14/4	Started "Voyage of the Dawn Treader"
20/4	Didn't finish, said it was boring and not as good as "L.W.W."
28/4	Tended to dominate in small group work on a sociogram
13/5	Able to locate words efficiently in dictionary - discussed use of thesaurus
24/5	Ghostbusters book (sharing) - needed prompting but then did a comprehensive oral retelling.

Sampling

Collecting and analysing samples of writing in any language-based area provides a wealth of information. If this information taken directly from the written product is supported by observation and interaction with the child during the drafting and revision of the piece, a comprehensive picture of the child as a writer and a reader is presented. The major elements which may contribute to this picture are indicated in the summary chart opposite.

There are three different kinds of writing which we systematically collect from children, viz:

- samples of their own choice of writing
- samples of a retelling
- samples of a proofreading exercise.

We fill out an evaluation sheet for each sample and then file it with the piece of writing (or a copy) in the child's folder.

In the following pages we have included some examples of evaluation sheets alongside the writing to which they refer, beginning with 'own choice' specimens from a Kindergarten child and a Year 4 child. Of course, because we knew each child and the physical and social environment, we were able to make some inferences which may not be apparent from the text alone. None the less we hope that the reader will be able to follow most of the connections that we made.

Material for evaluation? In Vonne Mathie's classroom children take responsibility for composing and scribing their own choice of text from the outset.

Name: ___

Text: (Child's own choice of topic, OR set topic e.g. read and retell) **Date:** ___

Meaning	Structure	Conventions		Additional Information
		Punctuation/Grammar	Spelling	
* Is it clear?	* syntax	* capitals	* spelling the way it sounds	*length of piece compared with previous samples
* Does it make sense?	* sequence	* full stops	*e.g. U (you)*	*genre and suitability of language
* Is the main idea developed?	* appropriateness of lead and ending	* commas	* spelling the way it articulates	*displayed knowledge of concepts
* Is sufficient information provided?	* Is the writing cohesive?	* apostrophes	*e.g. CHRIDAGEN (tried again)*	*evidence of spillover from other language experiences
* Does it need tightening?	* Are there guiding structures? *e.g. title, headings, subheadings, labelled diagrams*	* quotation marks	* spelling the way it looks *e.g. GAET (gate)*	*use of reference material
* Does it show recognition of audience? *(e.g. proper nouns Vs pronouns)*		* hyphens	* spelling the way I have solved similar spellings	*comprehension of text (read and retell)
		* dashes	* copying environmental print	*ability to reconstruct text
* Does it show an understanding of purpose (to explain, describe, argue, persuade, inform...)?		* colons	* using authoritative sources	*overt reading/ writing behaviour
		* semicolons		*handwriting
		* exclamation marks		*attitude
		* underlining		*development
		* tense		
		* parts of speech		
		* singular/ plural		

Observed Need: What is the child's most immediate need which I should address?

(Observed needs should form the basis of the class program)

Graham Dean
28 OCT

I am going
to the fete
to buy
sum candy-
flos and a
sho bag
and one of
my mum's
qyupe Dolls
fo my sister and
she loves it!

Name: Graham (K. Purple)   Text: The School Fete (own choice of topic)   Date: 28/10

Meaning	Structure	Conventions		Additional Information
		Punctuation/Grammar	Spelling	
• Composed text to express his own ideas about the school fete using — * environmental print * letter sounds * memory. • Illustrations supported text.	• Used one continuous sentence.	• Used hyphen eg. "fanDy-Flos". • Used apostrophe eg. "mum's". • Used omission mark. • Used exclamation mark.	• Copied environmental print eg. "fete". • Used letter sounds eg. "Quyupe" → cupie / Kewpie.. • Used memory eg. "I am going to the", "and one of my mum's".	• Enjoys composing text to express his ideas. He now writes the text first, and then illustrates it!

Observed Need:
• Immersion in print
• Planned demonstrations in both reading and writing → constructing shorter sentences — eliminating overuse of "and"

What is a Rainforest?

A rainforest is the proper name for a jungle.
A rainforest ~~hast~~ to have plenty of rain,
protection from wind. ~~and~~ good rich soil and
Rainforests need to have ~~plenty of~~ rain
so that ~~all~~ the plants get water to grow.
Rainforests need good-rich-soil so that
all plants ~~keep keep strong, hotthey and to~~
keep on growing. ~~and~~ If a rainforest ~~don't~~
~~& dosn't to~~ dosn't get ⟨enafe⟩ enogh
protection from the wind small and
~~yough youg yough~~ young trees ~~web~~ will
get bent ~~ofe~~ or broken.

Name: Peter (Year 4)   **Text:** 'What is a rainforest?' (own choice)   **Date:** 17/5

Meaning	Structure	Conventions — Punctuation/Grammar	Conventions — Spelling	Additional Information
* information is clearly written and easy to understand, with a simple explanation of the conditions necessary for growth * starts to develop main idea but runs out of information. Tends to concentrate on conditions for growth, not the nature of a rain-forest	* good introduct? to topic, though needs further development * repetition of information	* good control of simple punctuation * correct use of the apostrophe of possession * used insertion mark to add and re-organise information	* obvious awareness of spelling errors with good attempts at correction * logical approximations e.g (hast to) - has to	* writing is a spillover from science unit on rainforests in Term 1 * started after reading and sharing "Where the Forest Meets the Sea" (J. Baker) * good vocab : 'good, rich soil.' 'protection from' * obvious understanding of concept of a rainforest * 2nd report this term

Observed Need: Discuss use of sub-headings as organisers of information

Read and retell

Full details of the 'read and retell' technique can be found in Brown & Cambourne 1987. It is a powerful data-gathering procedure since it involves the student in predicting, justifying, arguing, reading, writing and sharing. And because it has an oral and a written component, it helps form evaluative opinions of a wide range of attitudes and abilities — as can be seen from the following sample, a retelling of a fable, 'The Mouse and the Bull'. (The words underlined are those whose spelling the writer doubted.)

One day a littel mouse was playing in a
farmers fild when he saw a big black bull
dozeing in a nather fild. Being the littel
rascel that he was he desided to play
a trick on him, so he crept up to him
and bit his tail. The bull was furess!! //
The bull jumped up and charged toward
the mouse. It was no use, the mouse
was foster then the bull. The mouse
ran into a hole in the wall. Know
mata how hared the bull he
coulnt make the mouse came out.
  ✓ well done

Name: Caroline (Year 4)   **Text:** "The Mouse and the Bull"   **Date:** 22/5

Meaning	Structure	Conventions		Additional Information
		Punctuation/grammar	Spelling	
* comprehension and recall of fable good * appropriate language * main idea is clear and developed	* fable format correct, though doesn't state the moral at the end	* good control of simple punctuation * appropriate use of the exclamation mark	* logical/phonetic approximations * spelling errors not always identified	* clear/legible handwriting * exceptional understanding of fables: she didn't state the moral because she thought other morals more appropriate, e.g 'don't pick on someone smaller' * enthusiastic * constructive in argument

Observed Need: Exposure to other texts which carry a message, e.g parables

Proofreading

Children in our classes are regularly engaged in proofreading: they check their own writing as a natural part of the writing process and they also proofread as a discrete activity. They do so because we feel it is important that language users develop an awareness of the conventions of standard English expected in our society whenever written work is made public. Moreover, along with knowledge of the standard forms, they must have strategies at hand for achieving them.

One procedure is to invite children to edit a text written by a child about their own age. We ask them what advice they would be able to offer. They are allowed to use any of the resources in the room except each other — we want to see what degree of control or expertise they have, independent of outside help.

Name: Matthew

Today
~~Today~~
Toady is a raine Desember day.
              rainy   December

The boyes and grils in K. Yelow
    boys   girls   K. Yellow

like to plaey in the puddles.
         play

Cows, dacks and pigs lick to
       ducks   like

play in the loule mud.
            lovdy

Name: Matthew (K Purple) Date: 4/12		
Text: Sentences using environmental print		
Punctuation/ Grammar	Spelling	Additional Information
	* 10 errors 10 identified 10 corrected	* used wall print, reference charts and books from classroom library to correct spellings * enjoys working quietly and independently
Observed Need: Demonstrations on the proofreading of texts which require corrections in both spelling _and punctuation_		

What can we do with all this information?

The strategies outlined provide a rich data bank for each child, giving us a wide variety of information to draw on when we are talking or reporting to parents about their children's progress, or when we are planning future programs to meet the changing needs of our students. It is information which gives a comprehensive overview of the standard of language work being done in our classes — a good basis from which to talk to supervisors. And, whether we finally use it to complete a report form or to send home a profile which summarises the child as a language user, we know that we have looked at our students closely and regularly, as they work naturally without undue pressure. Because each strategy is designed to confirm previous findings at the same time as extending our knowledge in other areas, we feel we can talk confidently about our students' strengths and any problems they are still encountering. We are convinced that it is unwise to draw conclusions from single evaluation procedures. Whole language teaching requires whole language assessment and evaluation; evaluation by one-off standardised tests has no place here.

Chapter Five

CLASSROOM PROGRAMS

A program is a document required of all classroom teachers. In NSW the Department of School Education states that 'a program must be:

- *relevant* to the needs of all students in the class
- *purposeful* in serving needs of students and curriculum
- an *accurate* plan of work to be covered during a given period of time for all students
- *regularly revised*, reviewed and adapted to meet specific needs
- *well-organised*, clear and concise
- *well-balanced*, covering all curriculum areas
- readily and continuously *evaluated*.'

Indeed, these would undoubtedly be the requirements of any educational authority. A program is, however, a very personal document because it is a reflection of a teacher's beliefs and understandings about children and how children learn. But although the format or presentation of programs will vary, common elements can be identified in all effective whole language programs which reflect student needs, community needs, departmental policy and school policy. These common elements are shown in the diagram opposite. They are all vital to the teacher's program, and each deserves a brief explanation here.

Rationale: this should be a statement of beliefs about language and language learning and their implications for the classroom learning environment. Our rationales derive from the statements made in Chapters 1 and 2.

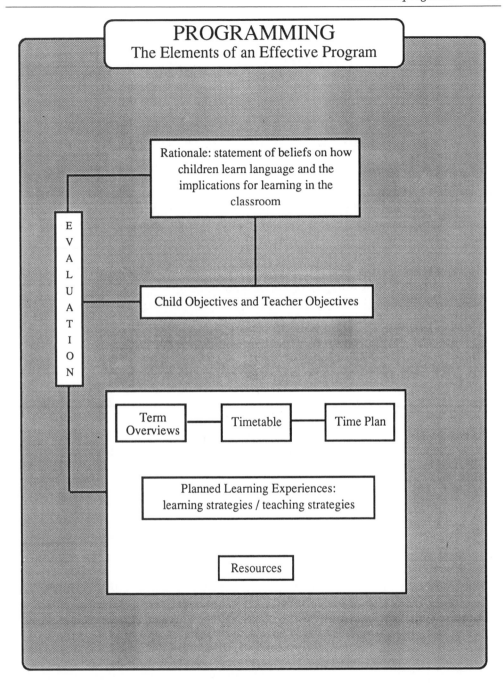

PROGRAMMING
The Elements of an Effective Program

Rationale: statement of beliefs on how children learn language and the implications for learning in the classroom

E V A L U A T I O N

Child Objectives and Teacher Objectives

Term Overviews — Timetable — Time Plan

Planned Learning Experiences: learning strategies / teaching strategies

Resources

Objectives/Expectations: these develop out of a teacher's values and understandings about language and language learning. They represent the specific expectations a teacher holds about helping children to gain control of language. Our expectations are wholistic, reflecting our belief that language learning needs to be whole language learning. They take account of developing positive attitudes towards learning, understanding the processes involved in language learning and developing the skills needed to control language effectively. We have summarised them near the beginning of the case studies in Chapter 3 (see pp. 24-25 and 39-40).

Supporting these expectations, there are language objectives in our schools' policies which list a wide range of fairly specific skills. We often refer to these lists when determining what needs demonstrating.

Overviews: these help to ensure that the program is balanced in its treatment of demonstrations, genre, resources and curriculum areas.

Demonstrations: we believe that children need to be shown the full spectrum of our language through both programmed and incidental demonstrations. By using a term overview we are constantly reminded of this range of demonstrations.

Genre: children need demonstrations from the range of genres they encounter in their reading. We map these in an overview to ensure that a balance is maintained. In K-2 the emphasis is purely on immersing young children in a variety of language forms. In Years 3-6 we would expect that children be encouraged to write in different genres in order to better understand the characteristics of each one.

Resources: schools with mandatory curriculum areas and limited resources need overviews to ensure that every class has the opportunity to use any of the resources it may require.

Curriculum: although the days are long gone of programming x number of minutes per subject per week, teachers are still accountable for providing comprehensive coverage of all curriculum areas. Within each curriculum area, overviews help to ensure that every component of the curriculum is given adequate treatment.

Timetable: any class timetable must take account of individual school and grade requirements. Here the range of variation is such that there seems to be little point in drawing up a 'typical' timetable. However, as we have said, it is highly desirable to incorporate an uninterrupted two-hour language session every day if possible.

Time Plan: we find that time plans for our language sessions are a great help in maintaining a balance between the different components, and that the children thrive on a predictable pattern of activities. Our language time plans have already been shown in Chapter 3 (on pp. 26 and 43).

Planned Learning Experiences: a description of sequenced learning experiences showing how information will be presented to children and how they can organise and respond to it is at the core of teachers' programs.

On the following pages we have included some examples of overviews and more detailed planning taken from our own programs.

Demonstrations Overview

Class: K Purple   Term: 3

AREAS of LANGUAGE DEVELOPMENT	1	2	3	4	5	6	7	8	9	10
Reading Process —										
* cueing systems	✓	✓	✓	✓	✓	✓	✓	✓	✓	✓
* alphabetical order			✓	✓				✓		✓
* predicting / confirming	✓	✓	✓	✓	✓	✓	✓	✓	✓	✓
* sequencing		✓				✓		✓	✓	
* choosing books	✓						✓			
* using reference material					✓				✓	
* sound/symbol relationships	✓	✓	✓	✓	✓	✓	✓	✓	✓	✓
* book/print concepts	✓	✓	✓	✓	✓	✓	✓	✓	✓	✓
Writing Process —										
* brainstorming	✓	✓		✓			✓			
* gathering information								✓	✓	
* scrounging	✓	✓	✓	✓	✓	✓	✓	✓	✓	✓
* developing ideas					✓	✓			✓	
* conferencing		✓		✓				✓		
* revising			✓				✓			
* proofreading					✓			✓		
* publishing					✓				✓	✓
Conventions of Written Language —										
* spelling	✓	✓	✓	✓	✓	✓	✓	✓	✓	✓
* punctuation	✓			✓		✓			✓	
* vocabulary		✓			✓			✓	✓	
* grammar			✓		✓			✓		
* tense										
* sentence structure	✓			✓		✓			✓	
* paragraphing										
* handwriting	✓	✓	✓	✓	✓	✓	✓	✓	✓	✓

AREAS of LANGUAGE DEVELOPMENT	WEEKS									
	1	2	3	4	5	6	7	8	9	10
Genre										
* observation/comment								✓	✓	
* narrative			✓	✓	✓		✓	✓		✓
* poetry		✓				✓			✓	
* information text			✓	✓	✓		✓			✓
* procedural text						✓		✓		
* recount		✓			✓					
* letter	✓									
* playscript										

Demonstrations   Class: K Purple   Term: 3

Focus: Reading Process		
Observed Need	**Demonstration**	**Date**
predicting/ confirming	* predict book content based on knowledge of author	27/7, 8/8, 30/8, 13/9
	* discuss storyline on basis of title/cover	19/7, 25/7, 9/8
	* mask text and predict storyline using picture clues	20/7, 26/7
	* omit one section of story. Predict omitted section, then reread entire story to confirm	15/8
	* mask certain words in the text (cloze) in order to promote the child's use of: • semantic • syntactic • graphophonic cues	2/8, 10/8, 23/8, 31/8, 5/9, 20/9

PLANNED LEARNING EXPERIENCES
K. Purple   Term 3 – Week 10
[extending work done on Monday and Tuesday —
based on Big Book "Woosh !" (Rigby Story Box)]

Observed Need	Teaching/Learning Strategies
Immersion in print Demonstration of what print does, how it works, how it is used, what form it takes	**Initial Whole Class Focuses** **Wednesday** Read (from O/Hs) and discuss the following poems about the wind — "The Wind" (Christina Rossetti) "Wind in the Dark" (Unknown) "The Night Wind" (Catherine A. Morin). **Thursday** Read and discuss the Norwegian tale, "The Lad Who Went to the North Wind" (from *The Arbuthnot Anthology of Children's Literature*). **Friday** Read and discuss the story, "When the Wind Changed" (Ruth Park and Deborah Niland).
	Reading Focus
Repetition of heavy duty words and sentence patterns	**Wednesday** Children are divided into two groups — Group A reads Big Book "Woosh !", with Group B repeating each sentence as echo. Groups then swap roles.
Choral reading	**Thursday** Children clap the rhythm as they read "Woosh !" together.
Shared reading	**Friday** Children read "Woosh !" together.

Observed Need	Teaching / Learning Strategies
	Group Activities
	Children are divided into three groups. Each group participates in one activity each day.
Repetition of heavy duty words and sentence patterns	**Activity 1 (with teacher)**
	Innovating on the text (Big Book "Woosh!") — I had a little _____. Her name was _____.
Responding to text through discussion and visual arts	Children use paint to illustrate the new verses on art paper.
	(Friday's group to compose new story ending)
Demonstration of reading for a specific purpose using appropriate genre	**Activity 2 (with parent)**
	Children read instructions (O/H) for constructing a kite. They construct kites following the instructions. They fly their kites in the playground.
	Activity 3
	This group divides into two smaller groups. While one completes the Listening Post task, the other completes the Letter Focus task. They then change over.
	Listening Post Task
Listening and following text	Children listen to and follow the text of the story "Bounce".
Responding to text through visual arts	Using coloured pencils, they illustrate their favourite part of the story.
Writing text which supports illustrations	They label their illustrations with appropriate text.
	Letter Focus Task
Recognising the letter "Kk"	Children complete "Kk" stencil.
Using correct movements to form lower case "k"	They then cut suitable pictures (e.g. kettle, koala) from magazines, paste them onto the back of the stencil and label with appropriate text (N.B. Children may need to take stencils home to finish them.).

OVERVIEW OF GENRE: 4B LANGUAGE SESSION

TERM	WEEKS	GENRE	FOCUS
1	1 - 4	Narrative	Fairytales
	5 - 8	Expository Text	Science: Insects
2	1 - 3	Expository Text	Science: Conservation
	4 - 6	Poetry	Free Verse
	7 - 10	Expository Text	Social Studies: Australian Goldfields
3	1 - 4	Narrative	Development of Character
	5 - 7	Expository Text	Social Studies: Bushrangers
	8 - 9	Report	Science: Experiment Format
4	1 - 5	Narrative	Development of Atmosphere and Setting
	6 - 8	Flow Charts	Science: Weather and the Water Cycle

OVERVIEW OF PLANNED LEARNING IN SCIENCE: YEAR 4

TERM	LIVING ENVIRONMENT	PHYSICAL ENVIRONMENT	MAN AND THE ENVIRONMENT
1	Characteristics of Insects		Simple Machines
2	Plants: How They Grow and Develop		Conservation
3		Forces: Magnets and Gravity	Using Magnets
4	Life in the Playground	Weather and the Water Cycle	

RESOURCE ALLOCATION: YEAR 4 (Term 2)

SHARED READING RESOURCES	CLASS		
	4B	4F	4S
Science: Conservation	Weeks 1 - 3	4 - 6	7 - 10
Literature: Free Verse	Weeks 4 - 6	7 - 10	1 - 3
Social Studies: Australian Goldfields	Weeks 7 - 10	1 - 3	4 - 6

Curriculum Focus: Science (Year 4) Content Area: Insects Term: 1	
OBJECTIVES	PLANNED LEARNING EXPERIENCES
* Listening for - pleasure - information	* Shared Book: INSECTS (Methuen) with emphasis on the layout and structure of expository text, the use of photos, diagrams and abbreviations
* Demonstration of report writing	* Modelled Writing: think aloud session, writing a report on mosquitoes. Text organised using sub-headings
* Gathering information	* Reading a variety of texts on a selected insect, note taking, summarising and sharing
* Observation - sight - touch	* Collecting a live specimen, viewing in observation box, listing its physical characteristics and behaviour. Consider structure and function. Drawing / labelling

* Writing - drafting
        - revising
        - publishing
	1. 2 × Read and Retell - 'Insects'
	                          - 'Life Cycle of Dragonfly'
	
	2. Report on selected insect

* Interpreting	* Sharing / discussing reports / observations / generalisations * Brainstorming criteria for reports → class chart Individual / group reflection → chart → ind'l reports

Curriculum Focus: Literature (Year 4)	Content Area: Descriptive Writing Term: 4
OBJECTIVES	**PLANNED LEARNING EXPERIENCES**
* Listening for: - enjoyment - storyline - descriptive language	* Teacher Reading of a) STORM BOY b) MAGPIE ISLAND } Colin Thiele * Discussion re clarity of descriptions and Thiele's use of similes to paint descriptions
* Discussion/Justification Comprehension/Interpretation	* Story Grammar Chart - looking at essential features of MAGPIE ISLAND * Sociogram - looking at interrelationships of main characters in STORM BOY
* Reading - sequencing - to identify powerful images	* Small groups of 2/3 to resequence the section 'rescuing the sailors' (STORM BOY)
	* Small groups - re-read sections of both books - list vivid descriptions - make into chart as focus for treatment of similes
* Writing - word pictures - similes	* Stimulus pictures of insects: describe as to a person from another planet
* Word study - spelling - vocabulary	* humpy Coorong pelican weather wilderness tussock remote stretch sanctuary wild

Chapter Six

THAT SOUNDS GREAT, BUT...HOW DO I GET STARTED?

It is important to realise that the understandings and practices which we have shared in previous chapters belong to a continuum of learning and have been developed over many years of application within the classroom. On the occasions when we have had the opportunity to talk to other teachers about them, they have usually reacted with interest and enthusiasm but have frequently remarked, 'That sounds great, but ... how do I get started?'

The response of some people to this question might be to start small, i.e. to select one component of a whole language classroom, such as SSR or Writing, and work on that until both teacher and class become familiar and confident with the approach. Gradually others could be introduced until all components are operating successfully. Robyn Platt describes a similar approach in *Towards a Reading-Writing Classroom* (PETA 1984).

However, this chapter embodies our response to such a question. We feel that the most important aspect of a whole language classroom is the integration of the language components, and that introducing one at a time detracts from the wholeness of the language session. So we suggest that you consider what follows, use the information to formulate your own plan for implementation and 'have a go'.

Should you find that things don't work as originally anticipated, then stand back and reflect rather than giving up. Maybe the planning was inadequate; maybe the ground rules were not understood or accepted; maybe the activities were inappropriate or not clearly demonstrated; maybe it was Market Day or you had the flu coming on ... Whatever it might be, evaluate, modify, change, reorganise — but don't give up!

Getting started in the classroom

Timetable

While designing your timetable around the inevitable school and grade requirements, you should keep these points in mind:

- do try to include a continuous, uninterrupted block for language daily
- activities during the language block may have a literature, science, social studies, art, music, health or PD focus.

Class program

Remember ...

- a planned program based on children's needs is essential
- the program should be structured to include all aspects of language you consider to be important
- there is no prescribed format for programming, but yours should be comprehensive and sequential
- children need a variety of daily activities which swing from receptive ones (listening and reading) to active/productive ones (talking and writing).

Time plan

The two different but practical time plans presented in Chapter 3 may be used as a basis for your own — we can guarantee that they work. However, if you are going to devise a different plan, bear these points in mind:

- writers need input and so it's better for teacher reading, demonstration, print walk and individual reading to occur prior to the writing session
- a consistent and predictable plan provides security for children
- silent times (5 minutes) are useful ways to start or end a writing session.

Physical environment

When arranging classroom furniture, consider the features of your time plan so that you have space for whole class focuses and sharing, group work and individual work, and areas for specific purposes, e.g. quiet area, paint area, listening post.

You should also ensure that all the resources the children need are kept where they can easily be found and reached. Equally, environmental print should be positioned so that all the children can read it and know where to locate particular items.

Social environment

The ground rules for classroom operation are directly related to classroom routines such as DEAR/SSR, whole class focuses, print walk, etc. Children need to know how they are expected to behave during these routines as well as when they are interacting with each other. This means that routines and expected behaviours must be discussed so that children fully understand and accept them. In addition, teachers need to be consistent in their approach to such behaviours. If you want children to listen to a story, then it's hardly sensible to have some of them sitting on the floor listening while others are wandering around the room handing out books. What message are they getting? Children in well-run classrooms appreciate that their activities are meaningful and that the routines are reasonable and necessary. They develop these understandings from their teachers.

Resources

A good whole language classroom needs to be generously filled with resources. Learners need writing resources which are practical, inviting and readily accessible. They also need print resources which provide good models and support for novice writers, and cater to their needs and interests. For, as Smith (1983) observed, 'It is mainly through reading that writers initially learn all the techniques they know.'

In Chapter 1 we spoke about helping children to learn the craft of the author, i.e. 'acknowledging what is done in effective text and using this text as a model.' To do so, teachers must provide plenty of good quality material from which they can read and demonstrate, and which children can read themselves. We now offer some ideas we have found useful in trying to supply these needs.

First, because many of your reading resources will be drawn from the school library, we strongly recommend that you talk to your librarian and get her advice. She is conversant with popular books, can recommend authors, and has an understanding of children's reading habits. You should always allow the children a part in choosing library books for the classroom too. After all they know what they want to read and can read. However, their selections should be supplemented by your own choices. It's also worth remembering that municipal libraries can be a useful source for topping up the collection of books in your room — many will provide bulk loans to teachers.

Second, to ensure plenty of variety (including variety of genre), you may find it helpful to bear the following categories in mind when choosing books for your classroom (whether they are on loan or not):

non-fiction, e.g. biographies and autobiographies, recipe books and other procedural texts, information texts to support specific topics, magazines and newspapers

reference material, e.g. atlases and dictionaries (of varying difficulty or detail), thesauruses, word books, encyclopedias, telephone directories

poetry, e.g. rhyming, non-rhyming, narrative, comic, anthologies, free verse

drama

books without words, e.g. those by Mitsumasa Anno, John Goodall, Jan Ormerod

traditional stories, e.g. fables, myths, fairytales, legends

cumulative stories, e.g. *I Know an Old Lady* (Bonns), *Old Macdonald Had ...* (Pearson)

repetitive stories, e.g. *My Cat Likes to Hide in Boxes* (Sutton), *Noisy Nora* (Wells)

interlocking story structures, e.g. *Each Peach, Pear, Plum* (Ahlberg), *Gossip* (Pienkowski)

historical novels, e.g. *Golden Pennies* (Farmer), *The Silver Sword* (Serraillier)

science fiction, e.g. *Grinny* (Fisk), *Skiffy* (Mayne)

realistic fiction, e.g. *Separate Places* (Klein), *Sadako and the Thousand Paper Cranes* (Coerr)

picture books for older children, e.g. *Wilfrid Gordon McDonald Partridge* (Fox), *Rose Blanche* (Innocenti).

Third, you'll find it rewarding to gather selections of books by the same author, because children will often stick to an author once they have acquired a 'taste'. Such selections are even better value if the author writes books which cater to a range of ages/abilities, because then even the less able readers in the class can share in reading and discussion of the author's work and may be led on to try the more challenging books.

Authors who write across a range of difficulty include: Alan Ahlberg, Margaret Mahy, Robin Klein, Roald Dahl, Pat Hutchins, Beverly Cleary, Colin Thiele, Shirley Hughes, Ruth Park, Mem Fox, Jenny Wagner, Judy Blume, Rumer Godden, Hazel Edwards, Morris Lurie, Michael Dugan, Christobel Mattingley, Tomie De Paola and Sheila Lavelle.

Author awareness can also be enhanced by an excellent series of posters published by Macmillan. The text by Walter McVitty provides valuable background material on popular Australian, international and classic children's authors.

Homemade resources

Ready-made commercial resources can always be supplemented with materials made by teacher and class. Naturally it can't all be done overnight, but during the course of a year you can accumulate a really useful collection of items, such as those listed below.

Anthologies of stories written by children and published in class are always loved by other children.

Individual alphabet cards and word-bank boxes support young learners as they develop a variety of spelling strategies for writing.

Class books of various kinds are also favourites, e.g.

4L's *How to ...* (instructional texts)

2R's *Favourite Fables*

1G's *When the Teacher Got Mad* (innovation on text)

6T's *Jokes and Riddles*.

Ring folders containing songs learned in class, or favourite poems; the sheets, protected by plastic sleeves, can be taken out individually.

Alphabet cards for individual use.

Writing demonstrations book; if a large book with blank pages is used for daily writing demonstrations, there is a record the children can refer to whenever they want.

Writing ideas file filled with cards which might carry:

- pictures from magazines
- story starters, endings, interesting characters or places
- possible topics for writing devised by the class
- formats for genres which have been demonstrated in class.

Plays pulled out of school magazines (as many copies as there are characters in the play).

Class Big Book dictionary made from a scrap book; the pages are coded with upper and lower case letters, and words and pictures are added by class members.

Class letter books, e.g. 'The Rr Book'; children paste appropriate magazine pictures into a large blank book, and then teacher and class construct captions which are published beneath each picture.

Word wall charts brainstormed by the children might contain:

- heavy duty words
- synonyms for overused words such as *went, nice, got, said*
- homophones
- similes, metaphors
- word families
- sentence starters.

Labels and instructions can be displayed at appropriate points around the room, e.g:

In this reference area you will find dictionaries, encyclopedia, thesaurus, atlases and telephone directories.

Welcome to 1H's room.

Wash your hands before eating.

Personal word banks can be made from takeaway food containers, marked with children's names, into which are put any words they need, or have learned how to spell, or have difficulty with, or ....

Class word banks

Character files begin with the children brainstorming words to describe the main characters in a story you have read them. These words are then written onto cardboard strips and pictures of the characters are drawn on other pieces of card to complete the set. Children now match words to characters, and as the descriptions can often apply to several characters, there may be a good deal of discussion and decision-making involved.

Vocabulary cards are a good way to develop the concepts or the vocabulary presented in a book you have read to the children. First, list all the words you want to treat and cut cardboard up into rectangles about 10 × 8 cm. Then print each word on one piece of card and its definition on another. These cards are good for a whole series of games such as snap, bingo or 'memory': the children develop their vocabulary and spelling and have fun doing it.

Old books written off elsewhere in the school can often be redeemed or reused. For instance, pages with pictures can be glued onto card for sequencing games, or added to the writing ideas file.

Sequencing activities are easily provided for if you photocopy part of a story (or a very short story) which you have read to the children and paste it onto card. It should be a segment which has a logical order, such as the description of an event. Cut the card into chunks of text that the children, in small groups, can resequence, which will call on all their reading skills. Rhyming narrative poems are a good source of sequencing material too.

Skinny books are simply thin books containing a story. They are made by pulling apart a much thicker book that children have been avoiding because of its bulk, and stapling the sets of pages inside cardboard covers so that they become 'skinny'. Use books made up of a number of self-contained stories (such as 'Paddington Bear' books) and try to retain one copy intact.

General knowledge cards with questions written under the same categories as 'Trivial Pursuit': e.g. Science and Nature, Sport and Recreation, History, Art and Literature, Geography. The cards are joined with a shower curtain ring so that more can be added later.

Maintaining the momentum

Teachers become learners as they endeavour to develop their understanding of how children learn and try modifying or changing their classroom practice so that it reflects that understanding. As learners they are involved in a series of problem-solving exercises, where feelings of uncertainty, bewilderment, frustration and inadequacy can all be experienced. If they are to persevere in their exploration and learning, support structures are essential, and we offer the following suggestions to provide them.

- Identify a 'significant other' — another teacher within your own school, or at another school, whose beliefs about learning are similar to your own, and who is experiencing success in implementing those beliefs in the classroom. Informal interaction can provide a forum for discussing difficulties, sharing ideas and celebrating successes.

- Team-teach with a 'significant other' if the opportunity arises.

- Indicate your willingness and eagerness to join in co-operative planning and programming sessions.

- Visit other classrooms and invite other teachers to visit yours.

- Seek out and become involved in a local language learning group where interested teachers meet to give each other support — again by discussing difficulties, sharing ideas and celebrating successes.

- Become an active participant in the school language committee.

- Create opportunities to get involved; for instance, offer to share an idea or an article which provides practical suggestions on a relevant topic at a grade or staff meeting. Be a giver as well as a receiver.

- Visit other schools. Most schools are now able to operate with a flexibility which can accommodate inter-school visits.

- Read professional articles and recommended texts, especially those which deal with specific problems you are attempting to solve. (Our own recommedations, offering different perspectives on whole language, are listed in the bibliography at the back of this book.)

- Subscribe to professional associations such as PETA and ARA.

- Participate in seminars, in-service courses and conferences whenever you have the opportunity to do so.

Peer support network

The classroom visits we have suggested can of course be organised informally, but they can also be the focus of a formal structure within the school. Beryl Wood, a regional consultant with the NSW Department of School Education, has described this powerful staff development strategy as follows.

A peer support network involves release for teachers to visit a colleague. Options include:
- release during
  - grade activities
  - assembly time
  - scripture
  - RFF (Release from Face to Face teaching)
- buying time through the Disadvantaged Schools Program
- executive relief.

A peer support network can provide visiting teachers with:
- support from their peers
- opportunities to see how colleagues approach similar challenges
- fresh ideas and new strategies
- opportunities to reflect upon their own practice. This reflection can lead to confirmation of present practices or an indication of the need for change.

A peer support network can provide teachers being visited with:

- opportunities for identifying and releasing their potential
- opportunities to share with colleagues
- a reason for reflecting on their own classroom practice.

The benefits for both groups of teachers are:

- opportunities for face-to-face discussions of issues, problems and challenges in a non-threatening situation
- professional growth
- enhanced motivation
- opportunities for peers to share and work together co-operatively
- mutual support.

The outcomes are:

- a greater likelihood of commitment to change
- the building of relationships between staff
- more effective teaching practices.

Finally ...

Q: OK, how do I get started?

A: As in all other learning situations, employ the conditions of learning.

Immersion — reading, talking to others, joining support groups and professional associations.

Demonstration — visiting other classrooms and reading.

Practice — having a go.

Approximation — you'll make mistakes, but remember they're a natural part of learning.

Feedback — from other staff members, support groups and the children you teach.

Responsibility — you've taken the first step, you want to do it and no one else can do it for you.

Expectation — be positive; if you believe this is how children learn best, then you will overcome setbacks.

Engagement — 'Eureka! It's working, I'm learning!'

BIBLIOGRAPHY

Butler, A. & Turbill, J. 1984, *Towards a Reading-Writing Classroom*, PETA, Sydney.

Brown, H. & Cambourne, B. 1987, *Read and Retell*, Methuen, Sydney.

Cambourne, B. 1988, *The Whole Story*, Ashton Scholastic, Sydney.

Cambourne, B. & Turbill, J. 1987, *Coping with Chaos*, PETA, Sydney.

Cochrane, O., Cochrane, D., Scalena, S. & Buchanan, E. 1984, *Reading, Writing and Caring*, Whole Language Consultants, Winnipeg.

Daly, E. (ed.) 1989, *Monitoring Children's Language Development*, ARA, Melbourne.

Goodman, K. 1986, *What's Whole in Whole Language?*, Scholastic Educational, Ontario.

Graves, D. 1983, *Writing: Teachers and Children at Work*, Heinemann Educational, Exeter, N.H.

Hornsby, D., Sukarna, D. & Parry, J. 1986, *Read-On: A Conference Approach to Reading*, Martin Educational, Sydney.

Johnson, T. & Louis, D. 1985, *Literacy through Literature*, Methuen, Sydney.

Johnson, T. & Louis, D. 1987, *Bringing It All Together*, Methuen, Sydney.

NSW Department of Education 1987, *Writing K-12*, NSW Department of Education, Sydney.

Parry, J. & Hornsby, D. 1985, *Write On: A Conference Approach to Writing*, Martin Educational, Sydney.

Smith, Frank 1983, *Reading*, Cambridge University Press, Cambridge.

Smith, Frank 1984, *Essays into Literacy*, Heinemann Educational, London.

Smith, Frank 1988, *Joining the Literacy Club: Further Essays into Education*, Heinemann Educational, London.

Turbill, J. (ed.) 1982, *No Better Way To Teach Writing!*, PETA, Sydney.

Turbill, J. 1983, *Now We Want To Write!*, PETA, Sydney.

Walshe, R.D. 1981, *Every Child Can Write!*, PETA, Sydney.